A Book of Tre...
for Florida and the Subtropics

Second Edition
Revised and Enlarged

Illustrations by

Erland Larson
W. Ernest Vincent
Maxine Fortune Schuetz
Joyce Allyn

A Geat Outdoors Book

Great Outdoors Publishing Co.
St. Petersburg, Florida

Originally published as
Dictionary of Trees: Florida and Subtropical
©1963 Fred Walden

Revised Second Edition
© 1996 Patricia Walden
All Rights Reserved

ISBN 0-8200-0414-6

Great Outdoors Publishing Co.
4747 28th Street North
St. Petersburg, FL 33714

Printed in the United States of America

*Cover photograph: Bare branches and flowers of Red Silk-Cotton Tree,
Bombax ceiba. See page 65 for description.*

Fred Walden, like so many Florida residents, lived his early life outside the Sunshine State. A native of Indiana, he was farm editor for a publisher there. This horticultural background and his "magic touch" with plants accompanied him to Florida, where for many years he served as garden editor of St. Petersburg's afternoon newspaper, the _Independent_, now defunct. He founded the garden magazine _Green Thumb_, which was highly regarded by Florida gardeners throughout the years it was published. Using the knowledge and experience gained during a lifetime in the field of horticulture, Fred Walden wrote the _Dictionary of Trees_ in the late 1950s. The book was a staple on Florida gardening bookshelves for many years, continuing to sell well long after Mr. Walden's death.

This edition of Fred Walden's book is a revised version of the earlier work, undertaken by the publisher with the consent of Mr. Walden's wife, Patricia. It retains the character of the original book, but places more emphasis on descriptive and cultivation information important to landscapers and gardeners. The selection of trees has been broadened to include more native species, too long overlooked as landscape subjects; for these, an indication of preferred site is given. Scientific nomenclature has also been brought up to date.

How to Use this Book

The purpose of this book is to familiarize the reader with a broad selection of trees often seen in landscape use throughout the state of Florida. It is hoped that newcomers to Florida and those with an awakening interest in horticulture and landscaping will find that it helps them to choose trees appropriate to their needs and desires.

Trees are organized primarily as to their type and landscape use. Palms are listed first, followed by pines and other conifers, oaks, various other shade trees including elms, willows and maples, exotic pest trees, flowering trees, and fruit trees. This ordering is unscientific but makes sense for the average reader, who is not likely to have specific knowledge about plant families.

The generally accepted common name of each tree is given in bold capital letters, followed by its scientific (Latin) name. Scientific names are composed of genus, species and, rarely, subspecies. If the tree's natural range includes any part of Florida, it is listed as NATIVE, and the habitat to which it is suited is given at the end of the descriptive paragraph following. EXOTIC trees are those whose natural range does not include Florida; deliberately or inadvertently introduced by man, these trees may be from other countries or elsewhere in the United States.

The botanical FAMILY to which the tree belongs is listed next. For the most part, trees in the same family are grouped together, but this is not a hard and fast rule. For example, because it can be invasive, the Surinam Cherry is listed with troublesome exotics. One of its relatives in the Myrtle family, the Bottlebrush Tree, is listed with flowering trees while another, the Guava, is grouped with fruit trees.

The ZONES in which the tree may reasonably be grown in Florida are given. These may or may not exactly correspond with the habitat described for native trees, since under cultivation some of the factors that limit the natural range of trees can be mitigated. That is, soil may be amended, supplemental irrigation and frost protection may be provided, etc.

Finally, each tree is described generally as to mature size and general form, appearance of bole, bark, branches, leaves, flowers and fruit (if any). Any interesting or unusual cultivation notes are given, as well as an indication of the tree's tolerance for frost, salt and drought. Illustrations are intended to give a general idea of appearance and some aid to identification, though this book is not intended as a field guide to trees.

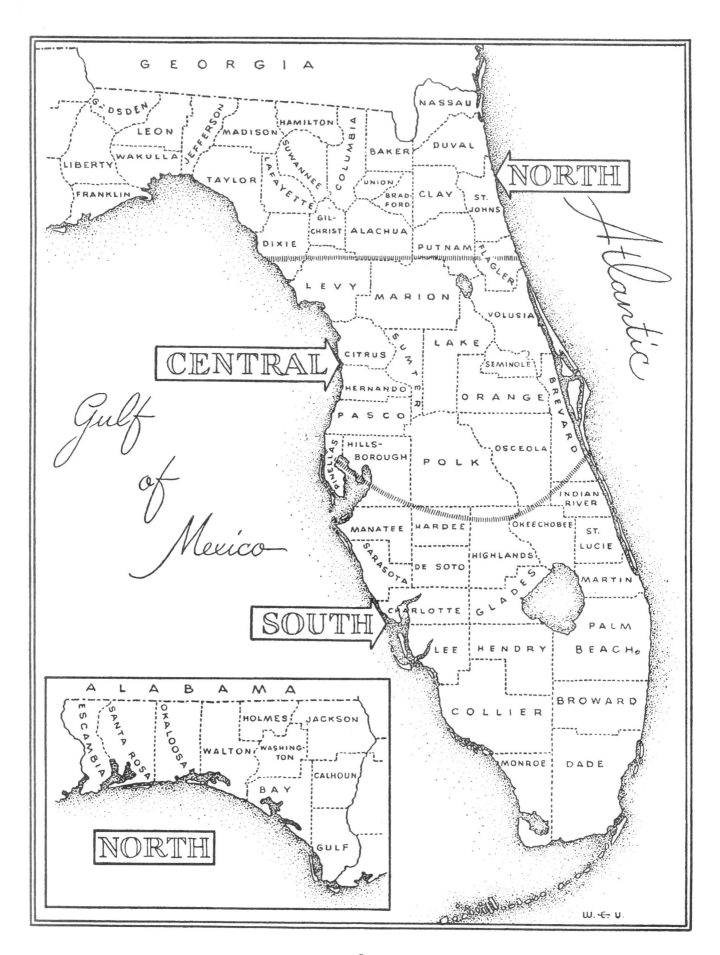

GEORGIA

GADSDEN
LEON
LIBERTY
WAKULLA
JEFFERSON
MADISON
HAMILTON
COLUMBIA
BAKER
NASSAU
DUVAL
FRANKLIN
TAYLOR
LAFAYETTE
SUWANNEE
UNION
BRADFORD
CLAY
ST. JOHNS
GILCHRIST
ALACHUA
DIXIE
PUTNAM
FLAGLER
LEVY
MARION
VOLUSIA
SUMTER
LAKE
SEMINOLE
CITRUS
HERNANDO
ORANGE
BREVARD
PASCO
OSCEOLA
PINELLAS
HILLSBOROUGH
POLK
INDIAN RIVER
MANATEE
HARDEE
OKEECHOBEE
ST. LUCIE
SARASOTA
DE SOTO
HIGHLANDS
MARTIN
CHARLOTTE
GLADES
PALM BEACH
LEE
HENDRY
BROWARD
COLLIER
MONROE
DADE

NORTH
CENTRAL
SOUTH

Atlantic

Gulf
of
Mexico

ALABAMA
ESCAMBIA
SANTA ROSA
OKALOOSA
HOLMES
JACKSON
WALTON
WASHINGTON
CALHOUN
BAY
GULF

NORTH

W. E. U.

6

Palms

Palms The family Palmae has over 2,000 species organized into about 200 genera, nearly all of these tropical. Most have a simple cylindrical trunk, a terminal crown of leaves which are either feather-like or fan-shaped, and perfect (having both male and female parts) or polygamous (male and female flowers separate) flowers. A few species occur as far north as the Carolinas; occasionally tropical species are seen outside the safety zone prescribed for successful transplanting. In general, larger, better nourished palms are more likely to survive cold snaps. Fertilization should be performed three times a year (spring, summer and fall) with a "palm special" fertilizer that contains magnesium, manganese, and appropriate trace elements. Among members of the Palm family, those with the greatest commercial value are the **Edible Date Palm** and the **Coconut Palm**.

EVERGLADES PALM *Acoelorrhaphe wrightii*

NATIVE: South Florida.
FAMILY: Palmae. ZONES: C, S

Also called Paurotis Palm or Saw Cabbage. This large, clustering palm grows to about 25 feet in height. Its natural habitat is the Everglades, but it has become popular as a landscape subject due to its ability to tolerate both wet and dry conditions. Once established, it is moderately drought tolerant; it is very salt resistant. It is cold hardy as far north as Orlando. Its trunks are covered with reddish-brown fiber and are studded with old leafbases. Leafstems are armed with sharp-tipped, orange teeth. Leaves are palmate, 1½–2 feet in diameter, shiny green above, pale green below. Small white blossoms are borne on separate flowerstalks in spring. Orange fruit about ½ inch in diameter is relished by birds. If left unthinned, Everglades Palm forms a huge, unruly clump. To keep this from happening, periodically remove the suckers which come up around the base, and trim away old leaves from mature trunks. Everglades Palm may be propagated from seed or by transplanting the suckers. FLORIDA HABITAT: Sawgrass marshes and wet prairies of the Florida Everglades.

ALEXANDRA PALM *Archontophoenix alexandrae*

EXOTIC: Australia.
FAMILY: Palmae. ZONES: S

Also called King Palm. This graceful palm reaches about 40 feet in height. Its trunk is 7–12 inches thick at the base and tapers to a shiny green, slightly bulging crownshaft. Feathery leaves 10–12 feet long have slender, bright green leaflets with gray-green undersides. Leaflets are 8–14 inches long and taper to a point. Leaf sheaths may vary in color from pale, milky green to reddish-brown. Creamy white flowers are produced in large masses and are followed by small, bright red fruit. Small, round seeds have a thin, fibrous covering. This palm requires loamy soil in a protected location. It is not salt tolerant but is moderately drought resistant. Young plants are easily injured by cold, but mature palms will survive short periods of below-freezing temperatures. *A. cunninghamiana*, another Australian member of the genus, is also tender to cold; slightly taller, it has a straight, slender trunk slightly swollen at the base. Its clusters of lilac-colored flowers emerge from below the crown. The red fruits that follow are about ½ inch long, round or oblong in shape.

7

FISHTAIL PALM
Caryota urens

EXOTIC: Asia and Australia.
FAMILY: Palmae.   ZONES: S

Also called Wine Palm, Toddy Palm, Jaggery Palm. Often reaching 40 feet tall, this palm has a ringed brown trunk 1–1½ feet in diameter. Unusual compound leaves are dark green and up to 20 feet long. Stiff, notched leaflets have wedge-shaped divisions resembling a fish's tail, hence the common name. Flowers are borne in axils of leaves, in large clusters of plume-like racemes. Fishtail Palm blooms only when fully mature. It dies after fruiting, but this may not happen for as long as 20 years; it flowers first at the top leaf axil and continues downward each season until the bottom one has bloomed. Reddish-black seeds are round or kidney-shaped. Fishtail Palm is not cold hardy and may be grown only in protected areas in coastal central or south Florida. Products obtained from it include sago (a powdery starch), fiber for weaving, and toddy or palm wine, a potable drink that is the source of jaggery sugar. *Caryota mitis* is a related species with similar foliage. Lighter green and smaller, it has a shrubby, clustering habit, rarely exceeds 20 feet tall, and lives longer; individual stalks die after fruiting, but not the entire palm.

PINDO PALM
Butia capitata

EXOTIC: South America.
FAMILY: Palmae.   ZONES: N, C, S

Also called Jelly Palm. This extremely cold hardy palm grows throughout the state and even into southern Georgia. Its striking, graceful leaves are blue-green in color and feather-shaped, with a characteristic backward curve. Leaflets are stiff but not spiny and stand erect from the leafstem. Though slow-growing, it eventually attains a height of about 25 feet. Its trunk is very rough, completely covered by the protruding stems of old leafbases. Green ferns, epiphytes, or other plants often grow on the trunk. Some people deliberately plant them there. Pindo Palm is very drought tolerant and somewhat salt resistant. Though its white flowers are not particularly showy, its round, orange, 2-inch wide fruit is very attractive and also edible, used to make a sweet jelly. Plant Pindo Palm in full sun away from buildings, so that its broad crown will have sufficient room to spread.

8

Native Florida Palms

Besides those described here, there are several other species of palms that are native to Florida. They were not included because they are too small to be considered trees. All of them are suitable for landscape use if planted in the right zone and microclimate.

Scientific Name	Common Name	Height	Zones
Rhapidophyllum histrix	Needle Palm	5 feet	N, C
Sabal etonia	Scrub Palmetto	4 feet	N, C
Sabal minor	Dwarf Palmetto	8 feet	N, C, S
Serenoa repens	Saw Palmetto	6 feet	N, C, S

BUTTERFLY PALM   *Chrysalidocarpus lutescens*

EXOTIC: Madagascar.
FAMILY: Palmae.   ZONES: S

Also called Cane Palm, Bamboo Palm, and incorrectly, Areca Palm. Grows in clumps reaching 20–30 feet high, its slender, yellow, smooth, ringed trunks resembling bamboo canes. Leaves are feathery, 6–8 feet long; light green leaflets 10–15 inches long arch from a yellowish-green midrib. Short clusters of tiny, white, fragrant flowers are borne close to the crown. Oblong and 3/4-inch long, the fruit changes from yellowish-orange to deep purple when ripe. Grown in south Florida as a landscaping subject and as an indoor ornamental elsewhere. Butterfly Palm thrives in rich, loamy soil. It is highly drought tolerant and somewhat salt resistant, but is easily burned by frost.

SILVER PALM   *Coccothrinax argentata*

NATIVE: South Florida.
FAMILY: Palmae.   ZONES: S

Also called Florida Silver Palm, Biscayne Palm, or Seamberry Palm. The common name of this palm comes from the undersides of its leaves, which show their pretty silver undersides when blown by the breeze. It is best used as a small specimen tree, as it rarely exceeds 15 feet in height and grows very slowly. Fragrant white flowers grow on a stalk which emerges from among the leaves in summer. The dark purple fruit is an excellent source of food for many species of birds. Silver Palm has fan-shaped leaves, deeply divided between leaflets, that are about 3 feet wide. It is extremely resistant to both salt and drought but is tender to frost. It prefers sandy soil and does not tolerate frequent flooding or mucky conditions. Though it may be propagated by seed, it is slow to germinate. Nursery-grown seedlings are available, but uncommon. FLORIDA HABITAT: South Florida pine rocklands.

COCONUT PALM *Cocos nucifera*

EXOTIC: Tropical America.
FAMILY: Palmae.   ZONES: S

Believed to have originated in tropical America, the
Coconut Palm is now naturalized in all tropical and
subtropical regions. Its height reaches 50–100 feet,
and it has a slender, arched trunk with a thick, dis-
tended base. Its graceful crown is formed by feathery leaves 15–20 feet long and 5 feet wide; leaflets
2–3 feet long and 2 inches wide hang from either
side of a stiffly arched midrib. Flower bracts have
sprays of waxy, ivory-colored blossoms; clusters of
nuts are borne beneath the crown. Older trees may
bear flowers, green nuts of various sizes, and mature, 12- to 15-inch long, 10-inch wide, light brown
nuts, all at the same time. Each hard-shelled,
monkey-faced nut is encased in the center of a fibrous husk. Aside from its commercially valuable
copra, the unripe nut yields a sweet beverage and
the meat is used as a vegetable. Commercial use is
also made of the nut husk, tree fiber, flowers and
roots. In south Florida, the Coconut is planted chiefly
as an ornamental. Annual rainfall of 40–50 inches
is necessary for healthy growth, so supplemental irrigation may be required. Propagation is by seed;
several months are required for germination. Com-
plete salt tolerance and high drought resistance
make the coconut ideal for coastal locations.

**CANARY ISLAND
DATE PALM** *Phoenix canariensis*

EXOTIC: Canary Islands.
FAMILY: Palmae.   ZONES: C, S

This palm closely resembles its relative the Edible
Date Palm (right). However, Canary Island Date
Palm has more fronds; its leaves also have more
leaflets, especially at the base, and they are more
pointed and recurved. Leaflets are bright green and
stand erect from a yellow midrib. Leaves may be
up to 12 feet long. Male and female flowers are
borne on different trees; they are yellow and grow
on branched flowerstalks that emerge from among
leaves in the crown in the springtime. Fruits are
bright orange, about an inch in diameter. They are
edible, but very unpalatable. Canary Island Date
Palm is sometimes called Pineapple Palm, for its
rotund, pineapple-like appearance when young. Its
barrel-shaped trunk has an attractive criss-cross
pattern left by old leafbases. A solitary specimen
can provide a regal centerpiece for a residential
landscape. When full grown it may be 40 feet in
height, though it grows slowly when young. It is
drought resistant, moderately salt tolerant and cold
hardy. Plant it in full sun with enough room for its
spreading, spiny fronds, and feed it regularly with
palm special fertilizer; Canary Island Date Palm
is susceptible to yellow foliage if undernourished.

10

| **EDIBLE DATE PALM** | *Phoenix dactylifera* | **SENEGAL DATE PALM** | *Phoenix reclinata* |

EXOTIC: North Africa and the Middle East.
FAMILY: Palmae. ZONES: C, S

This desert palm produces sweet dates in warm, dry climates. It often reaches a height of 90–100 feet, with trunks roughly scarred by the terminal bases of old leaf sheaths. Suckers grow up around the base of the main trunk. Leaves are 18–20 feet long and 2–3 feet wide, feathery and dark green or grayish-green with sharp spines at the base. Male and female flowers are borne in large clusters on separate trees. Fruit is an oblong berry with a grooved seed; a productive tree may bear up to 200 pounds of dates in a season. The seeds may be ground and used as a substitute for coffee. Propagation is by seed or by transplanting suckers when they reach about five years old; trim the top leaves back and plant them in a warm location. Though it does not fruit well in Florida's moist climate, the beauty, cold hardiness, and extreme drought tolerance of this palm make it desirable in the landscape. Commercial date growing in the United States was begun in the late 1800s in Arizona.

EXOTIC: Southeastern Africa.
FAMILY: Palmae. ZONES: C, S

This attractive palm is useful in the landscape, but only if planted a good distance away from walkways and regularly groomed to keep its spines well above people's heads. Each leaflet has a hard, sharp spine at its apex, which causes no problem as long as leaves grow at treetop height, 25–30 feet. If its site is carefully chosen and suckers are kept trimmed from its base, it can be a beautiful landscape palm. But left to its own devices, it becomes an unapproachable clump of thorny fronds. The trunks of this palm tend to lean at angle, hence its species name "*reclinata*", meaning reclining. They are covered with a reddish fiber which eventually sloughs away, leaving them bare but scarred by old leafbases. While this palm is related to the date palm of commerce, its fruit is unpalatable. It requires full sun, is drought tolerant, and can withstand salt spray. The bright green, stiff, feather-shaped fronds grow up to 8 feet long and add a tropical ambiance to the landscape.

PYGMY DATE PALM *Phoenix roebelenii*

EXOTIC: Tropical Asia and Africa.
FAMILY: Palmae. ZONES: C, S

This graceful dwarf palm is widely grown in Florida as a landscape subject, as a house plant elsewhere. Truly a "pygmy," it seldom exceeds 10 feet in height. Its slender trunk, 5–6 inches in diameter and covered with protruding, triangular, basal ends of former leaf stems, presents a pocked appearance at first glance. Arched leaves are 3–4 feet long with sharp spines at the base; drooping, fringe-like, dark-green leaflets are 5–8 inches long. Canoe-shaped flower spathes 12–14 inches long are borne among lower leaves. Small, greenish-yellow flowers are borne in clusters on short spikes, with male and female flowers produced on different plants. Seeds are about 1/2 inch long, oblong, with a small, sharp spine at the tip; they are seated, acorn-like, in a tiny cup. Though tropical, Pygmy Date Palm will withstand below-freezing temperatures for a short period. It thrives best in partial shade in loamy soil, and should receive fertilizer formulated for palms, as it is susceptible to nutrient deficiencies. This slow-growing palm is prized by many with small gardens or limited space; they can plant it secure in the knowledge that it will remain diminutive.

SARGENT'S CHERRY PALM *Pseudophoenix sargentii*

NATIVE: Florida Keys.
FAMILY: Palmae. ZONES: S

Also called Buccaneer Palm. This endangered palm was originally found only on Elliott and Long Keys. It became so popular as a landscape subject that wild stands are almost completely gone, most trees having been transplanted to residential yards. Sargent's Cherry Palm is small, reaching only 10 feet tall, and grows very slowly. Its gray, ringed trunk and smooth green crownshaft are similar to those of the Royal Palm, and its blue-green, recurved, pinnate foliage resemble the Pindo Palm's. Yellowish-green flowers appear in summer; beautiful, round, bright red, 3/4-inch wide fruit is showy at Christmastime and is eaten by birds and small mammals. Sargent's Cherry Palm is extremely salt resistant, withstanding even seawater flooding. It is also drought tolerant, but tender to frost. Propagation is by seed. FLORIDA HABITAT: Maritime forests of the Florida Keys.

| **ROYAL PALM** | *Roystonea spp.* | **SABAL PALM** | *Sabal palmetto* |

ROYAL PALM   *Roystonea spp.*

NATIVE: South Florida and Caribbean.
FAMILY: Palmae.   ZONES: S

R. elata (Florida Royal Palm) is a south Florida native, while *R. regia* (Cuban Royal Palm) comes from Hispaniola. The two are very similar in appearance, though the Florida Royal usually has a straighter trunk and grows a bit taller, to about 80 feet. Its pale gray trunk is often swollen at the base, with the upper, 6- to 10-foot crownshaft a light, glossy green. Alternate leaves are dark green, 12–15 feet long. Strap-like leaflets are 3 feet long at the base of the leaf spine, decreasing in length to a few inches at the tip, giving a feather-like appearance. Small, fragrant white flowers grow in thickly-branched, drooping clusters 18–24 inches long; they are borne at the base of the crownshaft (see illustration). Blue-green oval fruits are $^{1}/_{2}$ inch long and have a single, light brown, pea-sized seed. Germination occurs within several months and growth rate is moderate. Royal Palm will not withstand drought, salt or freezing weather. Wild stands of Royal Palm have become increasing rare. Removal by landscapers, development of its favored habitat and invasion by exotic plant species have seriously degraded its numbers. FLORIDA HABITAT: Subtropical wetland forests.

SABAL PALM   *Sabal palmetto*

NATIVE: Southeastern U.S. and Bahamas.
FAMILY: Palmae.   ZONE: N, C, S

Also called Cabbage Palm. Range extends north to the Carolinas. In its natural state it is generally found in large groups of closely spaced trees. Trunks are often encased by plait-like "bootjacks" composed of old leaf bases, but older and transplanted trees may lack them. The official "state tree" of Florida, this slow-growing palm eventually reaches 40–60 feet in height. Leaves are fan-shaped, medium glossy green above, grayish-green underneath, up to 7 feet long. Alternate, deeply divided leaves have drooping segments with thread-like fibers between them and grow on 4- to 6-foot stalks. Fragrant flowers are greenish-white and $^{1}/_{4}$ inch wide, borne in immense drooping clusters. Seed fruit is $^{1}/_{2}$ inch wide, round, and blackish-brown. The center leaf bud or "heart" at the top of the trunk was considered a delicacy by early Florida Indians and settlers. Unfortunately, removal of this tender bud kills the tree. Sabal Palm pollen also is the source of a delicious honey; it has a strong but pleasant flavor and is dark amber in color. Large Sabal Palms can be transplanted from swamp or hammock to the home garden, but this is a difficult procedure often accomplished with limited success. Many nurseries now sell trees that have been grown commercially, assuring better growth and conserving wild trees. Sabal Palm is extremely drought and salt resistant. FLORIDA HABITAT: Its tolerance for wide-ranging soil and moisture conditions make this palm a component of most Florida habitats.

QUEEN PALM   *Syagrus romanzoffianum*

EXOTIC: Brazil and Argentina.
FAMILY: Palmae.   ZONES: C, S

Also called Feather Palm. The height of the palm may reach 40 feet. Its straight, gray trunk is 12–14 inches in diameter, slightly larger at the base, showing rings of scar tissue left by shed leaves. Shaggy, spreading crown has feathery, gently arching leaves 10–15 feet long; leaflets are 10–12 inches long and an inch wide, drooping from a 2- to 3-inch wide midrib. The hard, woody bloom bract is 4–6 feet long, ribbed from base to tip; borne in lower leaf sheaths, it resembles a small canoe after it releases its golden-yellow flower cluster. Orange, inch-thick fruits are borne on foot-long flower spikes that grow laterally from a cane-like stem. When ripe and peeled from their fibrous husks, the hard-shelled nuts reveal the same "monkey-face" marking as a coconut. Dead leaves persist until cut away, or until fibers supporting them disintegrate. Queen Palm requires frequent grooming to prevent it from looking unkempt. Drought tolerant and somewhat salt resistant, it requires regular fertilization for best appearance. It is easily propagated by seed.

FLORIDA THATCH PALM   *Thrinax radiata*

NATIVE: South Florida and Caribbean.
FAMILY: Palmae.   ZONES: S

This small palm is highly drought and salt tolerant. It may be identified by the prominent yellow ribs that are seen between the leaflets of its shiny, yellowish-green, fan-shaped leaves; the undersides are also green. The narrow trunk may eventually reach 20 feet; this palm is very slow growing. It bears clusters of small, fragrant white flowers in spring. The Florida Thatch Palm grows best in partial to full sun, in sandy, well-drained soil. It is a threatened species. Key Thatch Palm, *T. morrisii*, is a very similar, but smaller, species that is found in hammocks of the Florida Keys; it is also threatened. The undersides of Key Thatch Palm are silvery, not green. Both species produce white fruit, 1/4 inch long and berry-like, that is relished by birds and other wildlife. FLORIDA HABITAT: Coastal maritime forests of extreme south Florida.

14

WASHINGTON PALM
Washingtonia robusta

EXOTIC: California and Mexico.
FAMILY: Palmae.   ZONES: N, C, S

This palm reaches 80–100 feet in height when mature. The trunk thins with age and usually becomes covered with a shaggy mass of dead leaves that resembles a huge skirt, giving it the nickname "Petticoat Palm." Broad, fan-shaped leaves measure 3–5 feet across, with leaflets arranged in "accordion-pleats" having up to 70 folds. Tough, thread-like filaments surround the outer edges. Leaves are borne on 2½- to 3-foot long, spiny-edged, orange-brown stems, first erect, then spreading and finally drooping. Branched clusters of tiny white flowers are followed by round, black seed fruits. Highly resistant to salt, drought and wind, Washington Palm flourishes throughout Florida. Its great height puts it at risk for lightning damage. A related species, *W. filifera*, is much shorter and has a stout trunk; it is not commonly grown in Florida.

A "palm" that's not a palm...

KING SAGO
Cycas revoluta

EXOTIC: Japan.
FAMILY: Cycadaceae.   ZONES: C, S

Cycads are a very old family of plants, some fern-like and some palm-like in appearance. King Sago, though palm-like, is a Cycad. A slow-grower, it seldom exceeds eight feet in height. Its trunk reaches 12–15 inches in diameter and is topped by a crown of dark green, feather-shaped leaves. Stiff and glossy, they are 5–7 feet long, with 4- to 5-inch long leaflets extending from the midrib. A large flower-cone emerges from the center bud; male and female flowers grow on separate plants. The yellowish-orange male cone is cylindrical; the female cone is smaller and paler in color and is more rounded and dome-shaped. Reddish, inch-long seeds are produced on female plants; they number 100–150 and have edible kernels. The Queen Sago (*Cycas circinalis*) is a native of the East Indies and East Africa. Less hardy than King Sago, it develops into a much larger plant, sometimes reaching 15 feet in height, but in all other respects is very similar. Propagation of King Sago is by seed, several months being required for germination. Both Sagos are moderately salt tolerant and very drought resistant. They are susceptible to nutrient deficiencies and should be fed three times a year with a palm fertilizer.

Members of this important family of evergreen trees and shrubs are characterized by needle-shaped or scale-like leaves and cones with woody, fleshy or membranous scales. Pines are evergreen; like all plants with that designation they are never without green leaves (needles, in this case). But they do lose their leaves, albeit a few at a time. Depending on the species, a leaf may remain for 2–4 years before being replaced. Pines bear two kinds of cones (called strobili) which are their reproductive organs, rather than the flowers found in angiosperms. One is the seed cone, ½–1 inch long, containing the female ovum; the other, gen-

Pines

erally under 2 inches long, bears male stamens with pollen. When the powdery pollen ripens and is blown away, the male cone withers and drops from the tree. The female cone comes in contact with the pollen, is fertilized, and continues to grow until maturity, the length of time varying with different species. Pines are very important economically, providing lumber and paper pulp. Unlike many trees, pines are very adaptable to varying climatic conditions. Their nutritional needs are small; most actually prefer well-drained, poor, sandy soils to rich loam.

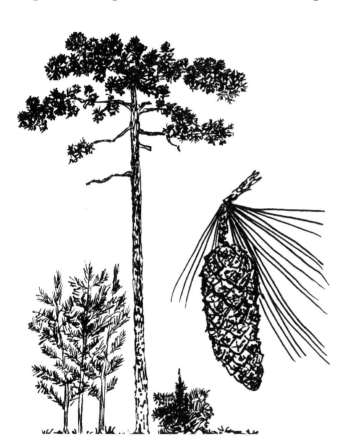

SLASH PINE · *Pinus elliotti*

NATIVE: Southern U.S., Bahamas, Caribbean.
FAMILY: Pinaceae · ZONES: N, C, S

Slash Pine is found all over Florida and the southern areas of adjoining states. A subspecies, *P. elliottii densa*, is confined to south Florida and the coasts of central Florida. A similar species is Cuban Pine (*P. caribaea*), native to Central America and the Caribbean, but naturalized in south Florida. Both Slash Pine and Cuban Pine are valuable timber trees, growing 75–150 feet tall. If they escape the lumberman's saw, they may live to be 200 years old. They produce the heaviest wood of any pine and historically have been a major source of turpentine. The Slash Pine is one of the most rapid-growing pines; this, combined with its copious production of fertile seeds, makes it ideal for forest reclamation. It is also a beautiful shade tree for landscaping or when used as a roadside planting. Huge stands of Slash Pine were killed or severely damaged by Hurricane Andrew in 1992. Many of the trees that survived the storm soon succumbed to attacks by pine boring beetles. Slash Pines are very drought and salt tolerant, and usually require no irrigation or fertilization. FLORIDA HABITAT: Pine flatwoods and sandhill forests.

POND PINE · *Pinus serotina*

NATIVE: Southeastern United States.
FAMILY: Pinaceae. · ZONES: N, C

Also called Black Pine. Height when mature is 70–75 feet. The 2-foot thick trunk has heavily furrowed bark with long, flaky patches showing the brownish underbark. Numerous short branches form a high, round, conical crown. Needles grow in bundles of threes, each 5–12 inches long. Flower cones are borne in spring. Short, stemless, oblong seed cones, 3 inches long, ripen at the end of the second year; they are ball-shaped when the scales open. Black seeds are about ¼ inch long and have light brown wings about ¾ inch long. FLORIDA HABITAT: Low-lying areas of pine flatwoods, northern and central Florida, south to Lake Okeechobee.

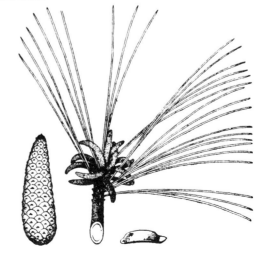

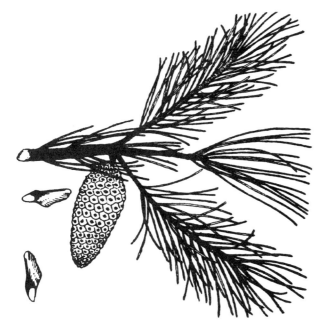

LOBLOLLY PINE   *Pinus taeda*

NATIVE: Southeastern United States.
FAMILY: Pinaceae   ZONES: N, C, S

Reaching heights of up to 100 feet, with a trunk up to 2½ feet thick, this big tree has gray, flaky bark with deep furrows that reveal reddish underbark beneath. Short, stiff branches form a broad conical crown. Needles grow to 9 inches long and are borne in triplets. Male flower cones, light green and 2 inches long, are borne in great clusters; female flowers are smaller, ½ inch in length, and are light green with pink tips. Fertilized cones ripen the following year, are 3–4 inches long with spiny tips; seeds are ¼ inch long, brown and black, with brown wings ¾ inch long. In Florida Loblolly Pine is most commonly found in the northern half of the state; it also grows in coastal Gulf and Mid-Atlantic states. It is not tolerant of salt but is drought resistant. FLORIDA HABITAT: Fertile, well drained areas of wetland and upland forests and pine flatwoods.

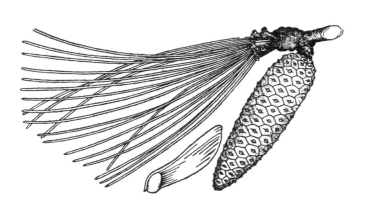

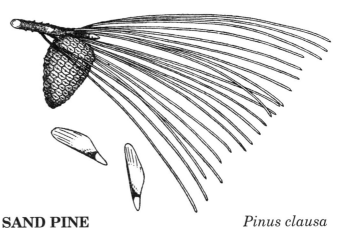

LONGLEAF PINE   *Pinus palustris*

NATIVE: Southeastern U. S.
FAMILY: Pinaceae   ZONES: N, C

Also called Southern Pine. One of the tallest trees in the Pine family, this tree may attain a height of 120 feet. It is an important source of turpentine and lumber. Its dark gray, furrowed trunk reaches 2½ feet in diameter, topped by a comparatively small and open conical crown. Needles are always borne in triplets; each is 8–10 inches long. Flower cones are borne in spring, the male clusters being 3 inches long and purple; female cones are ½ inch long and also purplish. Though not tolerant of salt, this tree is drought resistant and not particular about soil type, as long as it is well drained. (The Shortleaf Pine, *Pinus echinata*, is similar in many ways but is less common in Florida than in other states. Its needles are 3–4 inches long and are borne in pairs rather than triplets.) FLORIDA HABITAT: Pine flatwoods, upland mixed forests, and sandhill forests.

SAND PINE   *Pinus clausa*

NATIVE: Southeastern United States.
FAMILY: Pinaceae   ZONES: N

Also called Scrub Pine. This slow-growing pine reaches a height of about 40 feet. As its alternate common name suggests, it is undemanding both of water and nourishment. Dry, sandy ridges suit it well and it is also found along the coast as it is very salt tolerant. Its slender needles, about 3 inches long, are borne in pairs. Male flower cones are light purple, ¾-inch long and stemless. Female cones are smaller, about ¼-inch long; they are pink and grow on short stems. Fertilized cones ripen at the end of the second year. They are nearly 3 inches long and have reddish-brown, spiny scales. Seeds, ¼ inch long, are brown with black flecks and have ½-inch long wings. FLORIDA HABITAT: Scrub forests.

SPRUCE PINE   *Pinus glabra*

NATIVE: Southeastern United States.
FAMILY: Pinaceae   ZONES: N, C

This handsome evergreen has dense foliage which forms an open, conical crown. Its few short, slender branches surmount a tall, straight trunk which may reach 3 feet in diameter; it often reaches heights over 50 feet. The dark grayish-brown bark appears smooth; though narrowly furrowed, it lacks the characteristic plates common to most pines. Needles are about 3 inches long and grow in pairs. Flower cones are borne in spring, the pink-tinted male cones being about 1 inch long and growing in clusters; female cones are tiny, only ¼ inch long. Mature cones are 1–2 inches long and have spineless scales which open at the end of the second year to shed ¼-inch long, black, speckled, winged seeds. Spruce Pine grows best in fertile acid soil and requires supplemental irrigation during times of drought. FLORIDA HABITAT: Upland mesic hardwood forests; in Florida, these occur in the northern Panhandle and Big Bend regions.

BALD CYPRESS   *Taxodium distichum*

NATIVE: Eastern United States.
FAMILY: Taxodiaceae.   ZONES: N, C, S

Also called River Cypress, this tree grows to 100 feet. Mature trees have spreading branches that form an unevenly rounded crown; young trees are more symmetrical and cone-shaped. The straight trunk usually is swollen and buttressed at the base; it may reach 6–12 feet in diameter at the bottom. Thin, nearly smooth bark is reddish- to grayish-brown. Twigs have tiny, soft, green needles that grow perpendicular to the twig; in winter they turn reddish-brown and fall. In marshy areas root outgrowths, or "knees," emerge from around the dripline of the Bald Cypress. These are 2–4 feet high, conical at first but often developing into grotesque shapes. Knees bring air to the roots when the soil around the tree is flooded. Male catkins, 2–4 inches long, are borne on second-year twigs; female catkins are solitary and are borne simultaneously on the same tree. Round, green cones are 1 inch thick and are composed of angular scales attached at the center. Brown seeds are ½ inch long. Considering its preference for flooded areas, Bald Cypress is surprisingly tolerant of drought. FLORIDA HABITAT: Flowing freshwater and estuarine swamps ranging from extreme south Florida north to Delaware and west to Indiana.

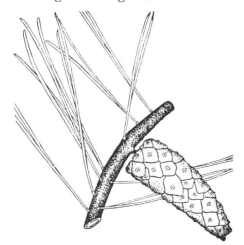

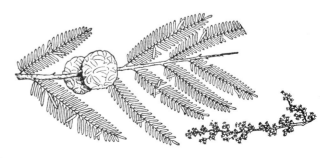

"Cypresses" & Yews

The **Bald Cypress** and the **Pond Cypress** are not members of the true Cypress family (Cupressaceae) at all; they are more closely related to the giant Sequoia trees found in the western U.S. The **Florida Torreya** and the **Florida Yew** are both endangered in their natural habitat. Like the Bald and Pond Cypresses, they have scale-like leaves, but their fruit is more berry-like, whereas the "cypresses" have a cone-like fruit.

POND CYPRESS
Taxodium ascendens

NATIVE: Southeastern United States.
FAMILY: Taxodiaceae.

ZONES: N, C, S

This swamp-dweller is similar to the Bald Cypress, but its height rarely exceeds 75 feet, its bark is thicker, and its knees are fewer. Leaves, $3/8$-inch long and awl-shaped, lie flat against the twig. Like the Bald Cypress, it is deciduous and highly drought tolerant. Seeds of both species are eaten by many kinds of wildlife. Wild stands of Pond and Bald Cypress continue to be depleted throughout Florida and elsewhere, for their rot-resistant wood and for garden mulch. Environmentally responsible alternatives to the latter are Eucalyptus mulch or Melaleuca mulch. FLORIDA HABITAT: Stillwater swamps and flatland pond areas in the southeastern United States, south to Lake Okeechobee.

FLORIDA TORREYA
Torreya taxifolia

NATIVE: North Florida
FAMILY: Taxaceae.

ZONES: N, C

Also called Stinking Cedar or Florida Nutmeg. This rare evergreen tree is capable of reaching heights of 30 feet, although the specimens remaining in the wild are much smaller. Its spreading, yew-like foliage exudes an offensive odor when bruised, accounting for its uncomplimentary alternate common name. Simple, narrow, tapering leaves are dark green and glossy above, lighter and banded on the underside; they are 1–$1\frac{1}{2}$ inches long with sharp-pointed tips. Male and female flowers and cones are borne on separate trees. Fruit is nearly round, $1\frac{1}{2}$ inches long, light brown, with two depressions at the base. Named for American botanist and chemist John Torrey (1796–1873), this endangered tree is found only in a few nurseries and grows wild in a very limited area of northwest Florida, near the Apalachicola river. FLORIDA HABITAT: Upland mesic hardwood forests.

FLORIDA YEW
Taxus floridana

NATIVE: North Florida.
FAMILY: Taxaceae.

ZONES: N, C

This evergreen tree reaches 20 feet in height, its purplish-brown trunk growing to 12 inches in diameter and surmounted by a wide-branched, rounded crown. Narrow, tapered, simple leaves have a leathery texture and are dark green above, lighter underneath; aromatic, they are 1 inch long. Male and female cones grow on separate trees; red, round, pulpy fruit, $1/2$ inch wide, has a single protruding seed. Like its relative the Florida Torreya, this tree is endangered in the wild and is found only in northwest Florida along the Apalachicola River. FLORIDA HABITAT: Upland mesic hardwood forests.

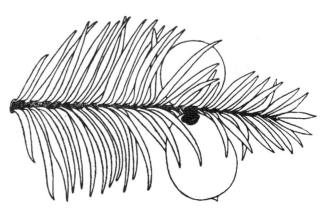

NORFOLK ISLAND PINE
Araucaria heterophylla

EXOTIC: Norfolk Island, Australia.
FAMILY: Araucariaceae.   ZONES: C, S

This distinctive evergreen can grow to a height of nearly 150 feet, its long, graceful, horizontal branches growing in distinct whorls 2–3 feet apart. Needles are 3–5 inches long, dark blue-green in color with lighter tips; they are sharply pointed and grow at a "V" angle, upright from the branchlets. Large cones are 5–6 inches in diameter. Frequently used in landscaping in south Florida, this tree is often grown in pots farther north. Although easily grown from seed, seedlings do not assume the symmetrical shape for which this tree is so admired. Instead, cuttings are made from the upper growth of young trees; these root easily, growing best in sandy soil in small individual pots—they should not be shifted to larger containers until well potbound. The new plants assume the graceful characteristics of the species when growth is well under way and can be maintained as container plants for many years. Highly drought resistant and moderately salt tolerant, Norfolk Island Pine is susceptible to damage by high wind or frost.

MONKEY PUZZLE
Araucaria araucana

EXOTIC: Chile.
FAMILY: Araucariaceae.   ZONES: N, C, S

This rather ungainly evergreen tree grows to 50 feet in height, with brittle, intertwined branches and brown, scaly bark. Leaves are dark glossy green, 1–1½ inches long and ¼ inch wide; stiff, with sharp-pointed tips and wedge-shaped bases, they grow close together around twigs, often overlapping. Its spiny nature gives this tree its common name: it is a puzzle even for a monkey to climb. It bears large edible nuts and is a close relative of the Norfolk Island Pine, but is much hardier. Grown throughout Florida as a specimen or shade tree, it also is planted in the open in southern England and Ireland, and in coastal California and southern Arizona.

GINKGO TREE

Ginkgo biloba

EXOTIC: China.
FAMILY: Ginkgoaceae.

ZONES: N, C

This hardy tree grows to 70 feet in height, its long, horizontal branches forming an acute, pyramidal crown. Excellent for avenue planting, it is deciduous, with leathery leaves 1½ inches long and 3 inches wide, fan-shaped with irregularly lobed margins and veins that radiate from stem to border. Flowers are borne in loose catkins and are followed by yellowish, cherry-like, foul-smelling fruit. Propagated by seeds, cuttings, budding and grafting, the latter methods preferable, to assure only male (and therefore fruitless) trees are used for landscape planting.

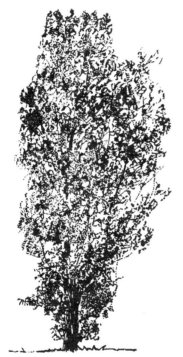

SOUTHERN RED CEDAR *Juniperus silicicola*

NATIVE: Southeastern United States.
FAMILY: Cupressaceae.

ZONES: N, C

The height of this evergreen tree reaches 25 feet. Its thick trunk grows to 2 feet in diameter and has thin reddish-brown bark. Sprawling branches turn up at the ends, forming a cone-shaped, pyramidal crown. Tiny, sharp-pointed leaves are aromatic. They grow in whorls around each twig in early growth; mature leaves, round-tipped and scale-like, closely overlap. Flower-cones are borne in spring, the male in great quantities, the female very inconspicuous; male and female flower-cones are borne on separate trees. Seed fruit is about the size of a small pea; smooth-skinned and bluish-black, it matures the following fall, the tiny egg-shaped seed surrounded by a resin-like pulp. FLORIDA HABITAT: Coastal uplands and upland mesic hardwood forests.

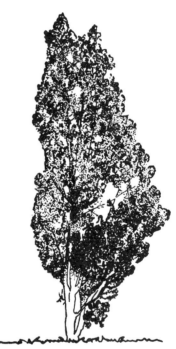

ATLANTIC WHITE CEDAR *Chamaecyparis thyoides*

NATIVE: Eastern United States.
FAMILY: Cupressaceae.

ZONES: N, C

Also called Swamp Cedar. This evergreen tree grows 50–80 feet high, with trunks to 2 feet thick, thin reddish-brown bark, and outspread, nearly horizontal branches. Tiny blue-green leaves, overlapping and scale-like, have pointed tips; they press flat against and encircle each twig. Very small flower-cones are borne in spring, both male and female on the same tree. Small globe-shaped seed cones are about ¼ inch thick; they have scales attached at center and ripen the following fall. Atlantic White Cedar is found in freshwater swamps along the Atlantic coast of United States, especially southward. Its soft wood is used for woodenware, shingles, posts, boats, etc. FLORIDA HABITAT: Cypress swamp forests and hydric hammocks.

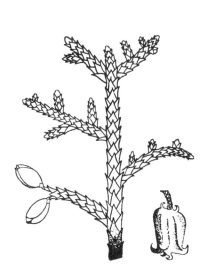

ORIENTAL ARBORVITAE *Platycladus orientalis*

EXOTIC: China and Korea.
FAMILY: Cupressaceae.   ZONES: N, C, S

Also called Biota and Tree of Life. This attractive, slow-growing evergreen tree is commonly planted as an ornamental landscape subject. Eventually reaching 30–40 feet in height, its short branches form a compact, cone-like crown. Tiny, light green, scale-like leaves are arranged on slender, vertical branchlets to form very dense, flat, lacy, fern-like foliage that is waxy to the touch and has a pleasing, balsamic fragrance. Small, spiny cones are about 1 inch long; each of their scales has a large "hook". Seeds are wingless. Propagation is by seeds or cuttings. This tree attains a diameter of 12–15 feet and therefore should not be used as a foundation planting. Its dense, low-growing, evergreen foliage makes it useful as a screen, either along property lines or blocking undesired views into or out of doors or windows.

JAPANESE YEW   *Podocarpus macrophyllus*

EXOTIC: Japan.
FAMILY: Podocarpaceae.   ZONES: N, C, S

This ornamental evergreen can grow up to 60 feet in height, but usually is pruned to more modest proportions. Commonly used as a foundation planting, sheared hedge, topiary, or specimen subject, its short, horizontal branches arranged in tiers and are nearly equally spaced up the slender trunk, in a manner somewhat similar to that of the Norfolk Island Pine. Erect, slim, dark glossy green leaves are lighter in color on the undersides; they are 2½–4 inches long and about ¼ inch wide, tapering to a pointed tip. Borders are smooth and the leaf is veinless. Leaves are attached to limbs and branchlets in a dense spiral formation. Male and female reproductive organs occur in separate flowers on the same tree, the male flowers borne on slender light-brown catkins about 1 inch long. Seed fruit is oval, about ½ inch long, with a powdery-blue sheen that rubs off when handled.

Oaks

At least 25 species of oaks are native to the United States and southern Canada. In north Florida they are deciduous, their autumn leaves offering muted shades of maroon and gold. Many oaks are semi-deciduous, retaining most of their leaves throughout the winter, especially if it is a mild one. Oaks grow in every part of the state, and their acorns provide food for birds and mammals. Even today, when homebuilders use many more metals and plastics in construction, oaks are highly valued for their timber. Oak furniture, floors, beams and ceilings give contemporary homes warmth and charm.

LIVE OAK

Quercus virginiana

NATIVE: Southeastern United States.
FAMILY: Fagaceae.

ZONES: N, C, S

This giant oak of the South is well-known in fiction and in history. Rarely over 60 feet tall, it may be three times that wide. Heavy, spreading branches grow horizontally from the short, massive trunk, which may be up to 6 feet in diameter and has narrow-ridged, brownish-gray bark. The evergreen leaves, elliptical or egg-shaped, are pushed aside as new ones replace them. While other oak species are also evergreen and could thus be called "live," the name has been reserved for this great, long-lived member of the Quercus clan. When ships were made of wood, this tree was so highly prized that in 1799 the U.S. government bought vast tracts of Live Oak timberland for building warships. It is prized today for quite different reasons: it is easy to grow, tolerates both drought and salt spray, is wind resistant, offers shade, beauty, and food for wildlife, and grows in every county in Florida. FLORIDA HABITAT: Rocklands, coastal uplands, upland mesic hardwood forests, and upland mixed forests.

LAUREL OAK

Quercus laurifolia

NATIVE: Southeastern United States.
FAMILY: Fagaceae.

ZONES: N, C, S

Reaching a height of 75 feet, the Laurel Oak has a round, symmetrical crown of heavy, upright branches. The sturdy trunk, 3 feet in diameter, has blackish-gray bark with wide, flat ridges. Deciduous to semi-evergreen, its leaves are simple, glossy green above with gray-green undersides; elliptical, they grow to 4 inches long and 1 inch wide and have pointed tips. Acorns are spherical, ½ inch long and nearly as wide, seated in thin, saucer-shaped cups. Fast-growing but only moderately drought tolerant, Laurel Oak is often used for shade and street planting. Compared to other trees, they are short-lived, with a lifespan of approximately 60 years. FLORIDA HABITAT: Wetland forests and upland mesic hardwood forests.

BLACKJACK OAK   *Quercus marilandica*

NATIVE: Eastern United States.
FAMILY: Fagaceae.   ZONES: N, C

Growing to 30 feet in height, this deciduous oak has a compact, oval crown of short, irregular branches, an upright trunk 12–18 inches in diameter, and coarse, black bark. Leathery, glossy green, wedge-shaped leaves have slightly downy undersides, grow to about 7 inches long and 4–5 inches wide. Acorns, single or in pairs, are ¾ inch long and seated in a bowl-like cup with thick, reddish-brown scales. Native stands, mostly in the Panhandle, often grow in dense thickets in poor soil. Because it is a relatively small oak, some choose it for planting where space is limited. FLORIDA HABITAT: Upland mixed forests and sandhill areas of the Panhandle and northern peninsula.

WATER OAK   *Quercus nigra*

NATIVE: Southeastern United States.
FAMILY: Fagaceae.   ZONES: N, C

This deciduous shade tree is widely grown in southern states. Its height may reach 75 feet. Heavy-trunked, it has large, upright branches that form a rounded, symmetrical crown. Bark is smooth and brownish-gray, with wide, vertical, flattened ridges near the base. Leaves are alternate, simple, dark green above and below; they are 4 inches long, 2 inches wide and egg-shaped. Acorns usually are downy, sometimes striped. They are broad, ½ inch long and grow in pairs or singly; they are short-stemmed and are seated in thin, shallow cups. FLORIDA HABITAT: Upland mixed and hardwood forests (especially near streams), and wetland forests.

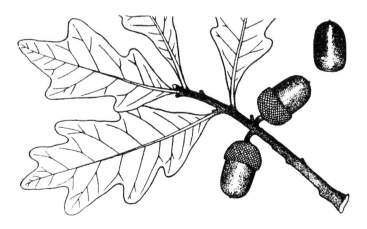

BLUFF OAK   *Quercus austrina*

NATIVE: Southeastern United States.
FAMILY: Fagaceae.   ZONES: N, C

The Bluff Oak reaches a height of 40 feet, with a narrow, open crown. Its trunk may reach 3 feet in diameter and has rough, flaky, grayish bark. Deciduous leaves are dark green above, lighter underneath. Only moderately drought tolerant, with even less affinity for salt, this oak makes an attractive, fast-growing shade tree when its need for water is met; in the wild, it thrives near streams. Acorns, broadly oblong and ¾ inch long, usually grow singly in thin, cup-like caps. FLORIDA HABITAT: Upland mesic hardwood forests of the Panhandle and northern peninsula.

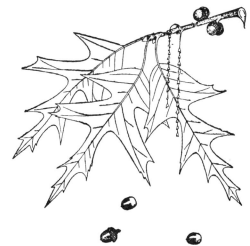

SHUMARD OAK — *Quercus shumardii*

NATIVE: Eastern and Gulf states.
FAMILY: Fagaceae.   ZONES: N, C, S

One of the tallest oaks, the Shumard Oak may attain a height of over 100 feet. Its trunk often measures over 5 feet in diameter and has grayish-brown bark with a crisscrossing network of flat-surfaced ridges. Leaves are glossy green above, lighter and downy beneath; they grow to 8 inches long and 4 inches wide, have a broad base and are usually seven-lobed. Acorns are oblong, 1 inch long, faintly striped and seated in a thick, downy-scaled cup. In Florida, this deciduous oak is usually found near streams in moist, well-drained soil. FLORIDA HABITAT: Upland mesic hardwood and wetland forests.

SOUTHERN RED OAK — *Quercus falcata*

NATIVE: Southeastern United States.
FAMILY: Fagaceae.   ZONES: N, C

This deciduous oak has a handsome, round crown with spreading branches. Its sturdy trunk reaches 2–3 feet in diameter, covered by gray-black bark with conspicuous vertical ridges. It grows to 80 feet. Leaves are bright green above, with yellowish-green, downy undersides; they grow to 9 inches long and most have 7 sharp-tipped lobes. Acorns usually grow in pairs; nearly round, they are downy, ½ inch long, and are seated in shallow, scaly cups. Southern Red Oak grows throughout the southeastern U.S., except for the southern half of Florida. FLORIDA HABITAT: Upland mixed forests.

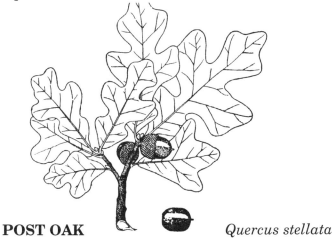

POST OAK — *Quercus stellata*

NATIVE: Eastern United States.
Family: Fagaceae.   ZONES: N, C

This sturdy tree grows to 50 or 60 feet, its gnarled branches forming a dense, broad crown. Its stout trunk has grayish-brown, flaky bark with deep, irregular clefts. The small, downy, faintly-striped acorns are a favorite food of wild turkeys, whose range often includes the dry, sandy uplands or rocky ridges that comprise the preferred terrain of this tree. Smaller birds and squirrels also feast on the acorns. FLORIDA HABITAT: Sandhill forests in Panhandle, north and middle peninsula.

WHITE OAK — *Quercus alba*

NATIVE: Eastern United States.
FAMILY: Fagaceae.   ZONES: N

A regal tree that grows to 80 feet, the White Oak has a rounded crown and a sturdy trunk that grows to 3 feet in diameter. Its ridged, scaly bark is very pale gray, accounting for the name alba, meaning "white". Dark green leaves change to red and purple in fall; they may be 8 inches long and 4 inches wide. Spring flowers are followed by acorns, usually in pairs; sweet, edible acorns are ¾ inch long, and grow in thick, warty cups. FLORIDA HABITAT: Upland hardwood and mixed forests of north Florida.

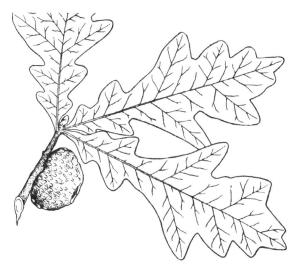

OVERCUP OAK
Quercus lyrata

NATIVE: Southeastern United States.
FAMILY: Fagaceae.   ZONES: N

Its height reaching 75 feet, the deciduous Overcup Oak has an immense open crown of large, irregular branches. Its short, twisted trunk has reddish-brown to gray flaky bark with deep, irregular ridges. Leaves are glossy green with grayish undersides, to 9 inches long and 4 inches wide, with sharp to rounded lobes. Broadly globular acorns grow singly or in pairs; about 1 inch long, they are almost entirely enclosed by the cup. In Florida, Overcup Oak grows mainly in river swamps of the Panhandle. FLORIDA HABITAT: Cypress swamps.

SWAMP CHESTNUT OAK
Quercus michauxii

NATIVE: Southeastern United States.
FAMILY: Fagaceae.   ZONES: N, C

Also called Basket Oak or Cow Oak, this tree grows to 60–80 feet. Its narrow, cone-like crown is formed by branches growing horizontally from a straight, heavy trunk 3–4 feet in diameter with shaggy, furrowed, grayish-brown bark. Unlike the Chestnut Oak of high, dry ridges, the Swamp Chestnut Oak prefers moist bottomland and is tolerant of considerable flooding. It is deciduous, with 8 inch long leaves that are glossy green with grayish, downy undersides. The large, shiny brown acorns are edible and sought by cattle (thus, Cow Oak). Its other common name comes from the use of its wood in basketry; the straight grain splits easily into thin strips. FLORIDA HABITAT: Upland mesic hardwood forests and wetland forests.

Scrub Oaks

Sand Live Oak, Myrtle Oak, Chapman Oak, Turkey Oak and Bluejack Oak sometimes are referred to collectively as "scrub oaks". Small trees with tough twisted trunks or branches, they are very slow growing. Because they have very low nutritional and water needs, they can survive in dry, sandy soil inhospitable to other trees. Along with "scrub pines" and other woody, shrubby plants, they populate high dry ridges, sand dunes and other areas with less-than-fertile soils. The largest such areas are inland, along the Lake Wales Ridge, but patches of scrub stretch along both Florida's Atlantic and Gulf coasts. Scrub oaks provide acorns, an important food for wildlife, as well as roosts and nesting places for birds.

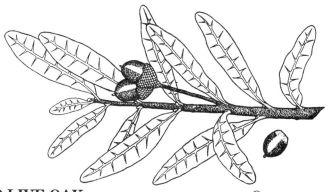

SAND LIVE OAK
Quercus geminata

NATIVE: Southeastern United States.
FAMILY: Fagaceae.   ZONES: N, C, S

The evergreen Sand Live Oak grows to a height of 30 feet, with spreading branches that form a rounded crown. Its trunk reaches 12 inches in diameter and has a gray, ridged bark. Leaves are bright green, heavy-veined with downy undersides; they may be 1–2½ inches long, their edges often rolled downward. Acorns grow in pairs on long stems; they are oval, ¾ inch long, seated in deep, narrow cups. FLORIDA HABITAT: Scrub forests, sandhills, and coastal, upland maritime forests.

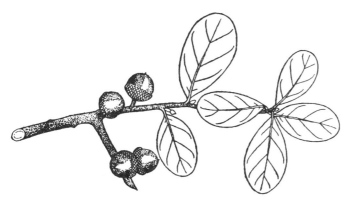

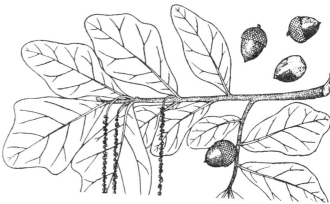

MYRTLE OAK   *Quercus myrtifolia*

NATIVE: Southeastern United States.
FAMILY: Fagaceae.   ZONES: N, C

This evergreen oak may reach a height of 40 feet,
its round, spreading crown and irregular, short
branches topping a twisted trunk with thin, smooth,
grayish-brown bark. Leaves 2 inches long and 1
inch wide have downward curving edges that give
them a cupped appearance; they are leathery, dark
green above, lighter underneath with hairy tufts.
Acorns grow singly or in pairs; they are nearly
round, ½ inch long, seated in downy-scaled cups.
FLORIDA HABITAT: Scrub forests of the northern and
central peninsula, and in coastal maritime forests,
where it is more shrub-like, forming thickets.

CHAPMAN OAK   *Quercus chapmanii*

NATIVE: Southeastern United States.
FAMILY: Fagaceae.   ZONES: N, C, S

One of the smaller oaks, this deciduous tree reaches
25 feet in height. Its broad, rounded, slender trunk
reaches 6 inches in diameter, with thin, scaly,
grayish-brown bark. Small leaves have 3 barely-
defined round lobes; they turn dull orange before
they fall. Acorns are egg-shaped, to 1 inch long,
usually single, seated in stemless, hemispherical
cups. Planted as a shade tree, Chapman Oak is good
for small lots and Xeriscapes as it is very drought
tolerant and grows farther south—to Lake
Okeechobee—than many of the other oaks. FLORIDA
HABITAT: Scrub forests.

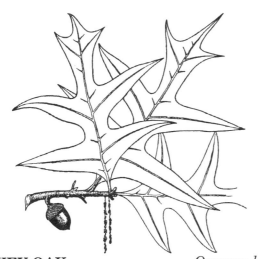

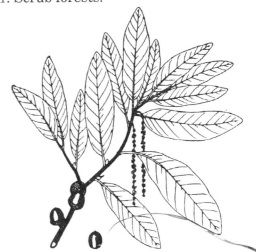

TURKEY OAK   *Quercus laevis*

NATIVE: Southeastern United States.
FAMILY: Fagaceae.   ZONES: N, C

The Turkey Oak grows to 40 feet tall, with an open
crown and stout trunk to 1½ feet in diameter;
grayish-brown bark has deep, rough, vertical ridges.
Leaves are bright green above, lighter underneath,
and grow to 5 inches long, with 3–7 lobes. Often
planted as a shade or park tree, this deciduous tree
is valued for its fall color. Acorns are usually single,
egg-shaped, to 1 inch long, and are seated in funnel-
like, incurved, soft, scaly cups. FLORIDA HABITAT:
Scrub and sandhill forests.

BLUEJACK OAK   *Quercus incana*

NATIVE: Southeastern United States.
FAMILY: Fagaceae.   ZONES: N, C

This small deciduous oak grows to 20 feet tall, with
crooked trunks reaching 10 inches in diameter and
having grayish-black, scored bark. New spring
leaves are tinged with pink and are downy; simple
and tapered, they grow to 5 inches long and 1 inch
wide. Acorns are nearly round, ½ inch long, seated
in shallow, downy-scaled cups. In Florida Bluejack
Oak grows as far south as Fort Myers. FLORIDA
HABITAT: Scrub and sandhill forests.

AMERICAN BEECH   *Fagus grandifolia*

NATIVE: Eastern United States.
FAMILY: Fagaceae.   ZONES: N

One of the larger trees of North America, 60–70 feet in height, American Beech has a round, dense crown composed of many lateral branches. It is deciduous, with a short, stout trunk that grows up to 2 feet thick; smooth, grayish bark covers the trunk and limbs. Deep green, alternate leaves are paper-thin but stiff, oval-shaped, 3–5 inches long. Male and female flowers are borne on the same tree, the male being ball-shaped, about an inch in diameter, and growing on a long stem; small female flowers grow in pairs and emerge from leaf-axils. Small sweet-flavored beech-nuts are edible; they are triangular, enclosed in light-brown, burr-covered husks which grow on a long stem. FLORIDA HABITAT: Upland mesic hardwood forests.

SILK OAK   *Grevillea robusta*

EXOTIC: Australia.
FAMILY: Proteaceae.   ZONES: C, S

This fast-growing evergreen tree is not an oak at all. Growing to about 50 feet, it has a thick trunk and short upright branches that form an open crown. Alternate leaves are silky and fern-like, 7–10 inches long; they are dark, glossy, brownish-green above with silvery undersides. Showy, yellowish-orange flowers are borne in one-sided clusters 3–5 inches long, followed by seed-fruits $1/2$–$3/4$ inch long. Silk Oak is easily grown from seed; greenhouse-grown seedling plants are raised for their delicate foliage, used in flower arrangements. Weak-wooded branches are often damaged by wind. Considered by many people to be a "trash tree," it is not recommended for home landscapes.

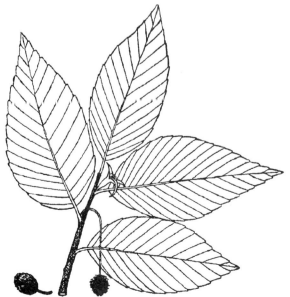

Trees and shrubs in this family are distinguished by alternate, toothed leaves and petalless, perfect or unisexual flowers. Most of the 130-odd species are valuable ornamental subjects, especially the Winged Elm, which is used in the southern U.S. as an avenue tree. New cultivars of the American Elm are reported to resist Dutch Elm disease, which nearly destroyed this species. The foliage of elm trees provides food for the caterpillars of Question Mark and Mourning Cloak butterflies.

AMERICAN ELM
Ulmus americana

NATIVE: Eastern United States.
FAMILY: Ulmaceae.
ZONES: N, C

The American Elm grows to 40 feet, with a slender trunk to 12 inches in diameter. It has light brown fissured bark and a dense, cone-like crown supported by long, drooping branches with smooth, slender, gray, irregular twigs. It is deciduous, with simple, alternate, elliptical leaves that are glossy green above. lighter beneath; they are 2–4 inches long. Each leaf has a pointed tip, partly rounded base, notched edges, and veining midrib to margin. Clusters of inconspicuous flowers on drooping stems precede new leaf growth. Thin, green, egg-shaped, hairy-margined, double-tipped, ½-inch long fruits develop as new leaves expand. American Elm is cold hardy and moderately drought resistant but not salt tolerant. FLORIDA HABITAT: Forests bordering freshwater wetlands.

WINGED ELM
Ulmus alata

NATIVE: Southeastern United States.
FAMILY: Ulmaceae.
ZONES: N, C

Also called Cork Elm, this tree grows to 25 feet, with a sturdy trunk to 2 feet in diameter and grayish-brown fissured bark. Its open crown has short erect branches. Twigs have distinctive cork-like appendages or "wings," which give this tree its common names. Leaves, flowers and fruits are similar to those of the American Elm. The seeds are eaten by birds and the fruit provides food for squirrels and rabbits. This deciduous tree is cold hardy and very wind resistant, but not salt tolerant. It is drought resistant, withstanding both moist and dry conditions. FLORIDA HABITAT: Wetland and upland forests.

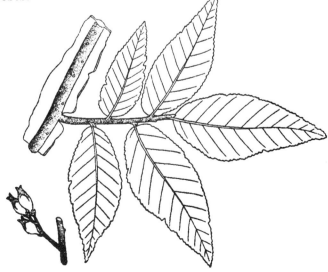

29

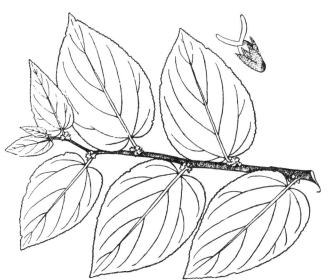

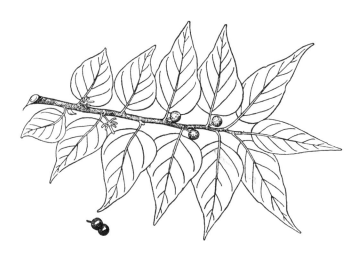

FLORIDA TREMA *Trema micrantha*

NATIVE: Florida, West Indies, Mexico.
FAMILY: Ulmaceae. ZONES: S

This small shrub-like tree grows to 25 feet and has a slender trunk 2–3 inches in diameter. Evergreen, it has dark brown, scaly bark and a narrow, round crown of upright branches. Leaves are attached to each twig in two vertical rows; they are dark green and rough-textured on the upper surface, pale and soft underneath. Small, orange, single-seeded fruits ripen in summer to provide an excellent source of food for wild birds. This tree is one of the plants that often springs up following forest fires. *Trema lamarckiana*, a relative from the West Indies, also grows in south Florida and has pink fruit. FLORIDA HABITAT: South Florida rocklands.

SUGARBERRY *Celtis laevigata*

NATIVE: Southeastern U.S. and Mexico.
FAMILY: Ulmaceae. ZONES: N, C

Also called Hackberry, this large deciduous tree grows to 80 feet, with trunks 2–3 feet in diameter. It has smooth, grayish bark and spreading branches that form a wide, round crown. Leaves are light green, simple, alternate, 2–5 inches long. The Mourning Cloak butterfly uses them as a larval food. Small greenish-white flowers are borne on new growth. Round, smooth-skinned, yellowish-red fruit ripens to bluish-purple; it provides food for a variety of wildlife. Drought tolerant Sugarberry grows on high ground in fertile soil, but also adapts to low floodplain areas. FLORIDA HABITAT: Hydric hammocks, maritime forests, upland mesic hardwood forests.

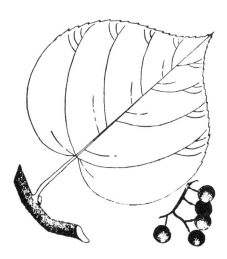

FLORIDA BASSWOOD *Tilia floridana*

NATIVE: Central and south Florida
FAMILY: Tiliaceae. ZONES: C, S

This handsome tree grows rapidly to 60 feet in height. It has a straight, 2-foot thick trunk, and attractive, broad, dark green leaves. Clusters of creamy yellow blooms appear in spring. Flowers are followed by woody, downy-covered seed pods; these small round fruits contain 1 or 2 seeds which ripen in fall. Its positive attributes have made Florida Basswood popular for shade and street planting, but with water restrictions the rule in central and south Florida, its lack of drought tolerance is a drawback. FLORIDA HABITAT: Upland mesic hardwood forests and hydric hammocks.

AMERICAN HORNBEAM *Carpinus caroliniana*

NATIVE: Southeastern United States.
FAMILY: Betulaceae.   ZONES: N, C

This small hardwood tree attains a height of 20–30 feet. Its slender, crooked branches and wiry, zig-zagged twigs form a widespread crown. The blue-green leaves are thin and have conspicuous midrib and veins. It is known locally by two descriptive common names: Water Beech because it grows most frequently near streams, and Ironwood, because its wood is extremely hard and strong. The wood is of little use as lumber, however, because the trunks are so short and are often crooked or twisted. This deciduous tree is extremely resistant to wind, and as an understory woodland tree prefers some shade. Greenish male and female flower catkins are borne on the same tree and appear simultaneously with new spring leaves; female catkins have a purplish tip. Fruits resemble fluted nuts; they are about 1/2 inch long and are attached to a three-lobed, leaf-like husk. FLORIDA HABITAT: Hydric hammocks.

EASTERN HOPHORNBEAM *Ostrya virginiana*

NATIVE: Eastern United States.
FAMILY: Betulaceae   ZONES: N, C

Like its relative the American Hornbeam, this slow-growing tree is sometimes called Ironwood for its very hard wood. The pale whitish-brown bark on the trunk is characteristic of trees in the Birch family. Foliage turns yellow and sheds in the autumn. Male and female flower catkins are borne on the same tree, in early spring. Greenish, nut-like fruits are borne in bladdery husks attached one to the other, cone-fashion. The "hop" in this tree's name is for the resemblance of the husks to the fruit of the hop vine, used in making beer. It shares with the American Hornbeam its wind resistance and small size, as it rarely exceeds 25 feet. A notable difference in the two trees is their requirement for water: American Hornbeam is a thirsty tree, while Eastern Hophornbeam grows in high, dry thickets, making it a good choice for Xeriscaping. FLORIDA HABITAT: Upland mesic hardwood forests.

HAZEL ALDER — *Alnus serrulata*

NATIVE: Eastern United States.
FAMILY: Betulaceae.   ZONES: N, C

This shrub-like, deciduous tree seldom exceeds 25 feet in height. It has an irregular, sparse crown and a slender trunk with smooth, thin, grayish bark. Leaves are alternate, dark green on both sides, 1½–4 inches long, oval with bluntly pointed tips and wedge-shaped bases. Prominent veins extend from midrib to wavy, finely-toothed margins. Hazel Alder is cold hardy and though not salt or drought resistant, it is tolerant of wet sites. FLORIDA HABITAT: Wetland forests along riverbanks.

RIVER BIRCH — *Betula nigra*

NATIVE: Eastern United States.
FAMILY: Betulaceae.   ZONES: N, C

This moisture-loving, deciduous tree reaches 50–60 feet in height and has a short trunk and irregular crown composed of large, upright, spreading branches. Its ragged, papery bark is characteristic of its family; on this species it is orange-red with a silvery sheen, darkening to almost black at the base of the trunk. Leaves are alternate, bright green, about 2½ inches long and egg-shaped, with a sharp-pointed tip, wedge-shaped base, and veining midrib to margin. The sharp-toothed margin extends at vein extremities. Flowers, called catkins, are borne in spring. The drooping male blossoms grow in pairs or triples, are about 3 inches long and are borne at the tip of twigs. Half-inch long, erect female flowers appear a few inches below. Cold hardy, but not salt or drought resistant, River Birch is tolerant of wet sites. FLORIDA HABITAT: Wetland forests along riverbanks.

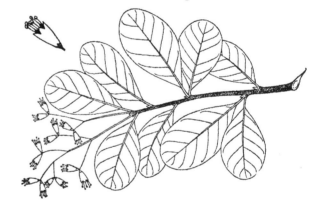

BLOLLY — *Guapira discolor*

NATIVE: South Florida and West Indies.
FAMILY: Nyctaginaceae.   ZONES: S

This evergreen tropical tree often reaches 50 feet in height. Its heavy, spreading branches form a dense rounded crown. The stout trunk, about 2 feet in diameter, has flaky, reddish-brown bark. Leaves are fleshy and egg-shaped, with round tips and wedge-like bases; they are 1–2 inches long, smooth with thickened margins, light green above, pale below. Sparse clusters of inconspicuous, greenish-yellow flowers are borne in fall in on long stalks. This tree and its close relative, *G. longifolia*, the Long-Leafed Blolly, are good small shade trees for south Florida; both are very drought resistant and moderately salt tolerant. FLORIDA HABITAT: South Florida rocklands and maritime forests.

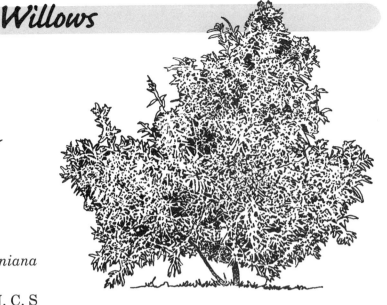

COASTAL PLAIN WILLOW *Salix caroliniana*

NATIVE: Southeastern United States.
FAMILY: Saliceae.   ZONES: N, C, S

This small, upright, fast-growing, evergreen tree reaches 30 feet in height. It has uneven, rounded crown of slender, upright branches and a short, usually slanting trunk with rough black, ridged bark. Bright, light-green leaves have silvery-gray undersides. They are alternate, lanceolate, about 5 inches long and ½ inch wide, with veining extending from the midrib to the finely-toothed margin. Catkins are 1½–2 inches long, borne in spring. Male and female flowers are borne on separate trees, the male flowers having bright yellow stamens. Egg-shaped fruits about ¼-inch long are borne on long stems and ripen in early summer, discharging tiny seeds attached by long, silky threads. Not drought, salt or wind resistant. FLORIDA HABITAT: Wetland forests along streams and lake banks.

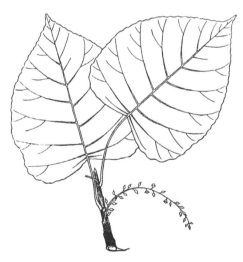

EASTERN COTTONWOOD *Populus deltoides*

NATIVE: Eastern United States.
FAMILY: Saliceae.   ZONES: N, C

This large broad-crowned tree may attain 100 feet in height. It has heavy spreading branches, short but massive trunks, and coarse gray bark. It is deciduous, with leaves that are bright green above, paler beneath. They are alternately arranged, 6–7 inches long and about 5 inches wide. Male and female flower catkins are borne on separate trees; male flowers are about 3 inches long, female flowers 5 inches long. Small, green, pointed fruits are less than an inch long and are borne on foot-long spikes. Ripe seeds are light brown and have tufts of white hair-like threads which eventually fall away. Infrequently cultivated in Florida as a landscape subject, Eastern Cottonwood is seldom found in Florida outside its natural range in the Panhandle. FLORIDA HABITAT: Wetland forests, primarily along the Apalachicola River.

33

FLORIDA MAPLE *Acer saccharum floridanum*

Native: Southeastern United States.
Family: Aceraceae. Zones: N, C

This ornamental hardwood tree is deciduous. It grows to a height of 60 feet, its dense crown supported by slender, upright, spreading branches. Tall, straight trunks have smooth gray bark that is usually marked with rough-edged, shallow, vertical furrows. Leaves are 2½–4 inches in length, slightly broader than long. Leaves turn yellow and scarlet before dying, often clinging to the tree until late winter or early spring. Clusters of tiny yellowish-green flowers are borne in spring on long stems at tips of twigs. These are soon followed by pairs of round, brown, winged seeds on thread-like stems, disseminated by the wind. This fast-growing tree is not salt resistant but is moderately drought tolerant. Florida habitat: Upland mesic hardwood forests.

SYCAMORE *Platanus occidentalis*

Native: Eastern United States.
Family: Platanaceae. Zones: N

Extensively used for avenue and park plantings and occasionally in home landscapes, this tree loses points for low drought tolerance. It often attains a height of over 100 feet, with immense trunks 3–5 feet thick at the base. The broad, open crown is composed of massive, spreading branches. Smooth, gray-brown outer bark is unable to expand as fast as the growing trunk; it breaks and peels in thick, irregular patches, exposing yellowish-white inner bark. Leaves, about 5 inches wide, turn yellow and drop in fall. Flowers are borne in spring: ball-like, reddish male blossoms grow on long stems from the bases of leaf stalks, while smaller, pale green, round-headed, female flowers cling to the ends of twigs. Pods ripen in fall and resemble small balls tied with string. Florida range is limited to western Panhandle. Florida habitat: Hydric hammocks.

SWEETGUM   *Liquidambar styraciflua*

NATIVE: Eastern United States.
FAMILY: Hamamelidaceae.   ZONES: N, C, S

These massive trees sometimes grow to 100 feet in height; trunks may be over 4 feet in diameter and are covered with deeply fissured bark. The bright green, 5-inch wide leaves turn red and drop in autumn. Corky wings or ridges appear along twigs and small branches. Flowers of both sexes occur on the same tree. The female flowers form ball-shaped clusters which develop seeds, turn brown and hang on into winter. The seeds are a good source of food for many bird species. Moisture-loving Sweetgum is often found on river banks, but also grows on higher ground and can tolerate considerable drought. FLORIDA HABITAT: Upland mixed forests, upland mesic hardwood forests and hydric hammocks.

WITCH HAZEL   *Hamamelis virginiana*

NATIVE: Eastern United States and Canada.
FAMILY: Hamamelidaceae.   ZONES: N, C

This small, bushy, deciduous tree is found in low wooded areas as far south as central Florida. It reaches 15–20 feet in height, with a broad crown of upright spreading branches and a long straight trunk 8–12 inches thick, covered by smooth whitish-brown bark. Leaves, 2–6 inches long, are a dull green; they are oval, with prominent veins and wavy margins. They turn pale yellow and are shed in fall, after which small yellow flowers appear. The bark and leaves of this tree contain an extract which is distilled in alcohol and used as a topical astringent. FLORIDA HABITAT: Upland mesic hardwood forests.

SHINING SUMAC   *Rhus copallina*

NATIVE: Southeastern United States.
FAMILY: Anacardiaceae.   ZONES: N, C, S

Also called Winged Sumac, for the flat, wing-like appendages along the leafstem, similar in appearance to those of the Winged Elm. Shining Sumac is a shrub or small tree that is deciduous, with shiny, deep green, lance-shaped leaflets turning red in autumn. Its tiny, hairy, dull red berries also provide late fall and winter color, as well as food for birds and other wildlife; they are borne in panicles at the end of flowerstalks. The green flowers that precede them are insignificant. Shining Sumac reaches 10–25 feet in height, assuming a shrubby form if the numerous suckers that come up around the base are allowed to persist. Though very drought resistant, it will also tolerate occasional flooding. It is fast growing, requires full sun and little or no fertilizer, but is not salt tolerant. Propagated by cuttings or seeds (often spread by birds), Shining Sumac can become invasive. FLORIDA HABITAT: Pine flatwoods and seasonally flooded prairies.

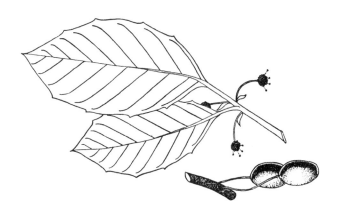

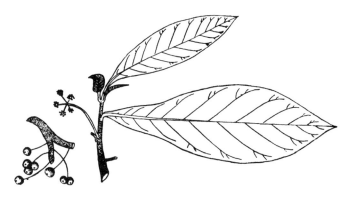

WATER TUPELO   *Nyssa aquatica*

NATIVE: Southeastern United States.
FAMILY: Nyssacecae.   ZONES: N, C, S

Water Tupelo usually is found growing in low,
swampy areas and along river banks. It reaches a
height of 100 feet, its large spreading branches
forming a compact, rounded crown. Tall, straight,
heavy trunks are greatly swollen at the base, which
is submerged in water much of the year. Dark green
leaves are 5–9 inches long, turn brilliant orange-
red in fall before shedding. Small greenish-white
flowers are borne in spring after new leaves are
fully grown. These are sought by bees, from which
comes the "tupelo honey" sold commercially in the
South. Male and female blossoms are produced on
different trees. Purplish, egg-shaped, solitary fruits
are shorter than their stems and are a favorite food
of wildlife. FLORIDA HABITAT: Cypress swamps and
hardwood swamp forests.

BLACK TUPELO   *Nyssa sylvatica*

NATIVE: Eastern United States.
FAMILY: Nyssaceae.   ZONES: N, C

Also called Black Gum, Sour Gum, and Pepperidge.
This large tree commonly is found in swampy areas of north Florida and reaches 60–80 feet in
height. Its crown, usually narrow but rounded if
growing in an open area, has spreading branches
supported by a straight trunk covered with rough,
gray bark. Leaves are 2–5 inches long and similar
to those of the Water Tupelo, though smaller and
with silvery-green undersides; they turn bright
scarlet in autumn before shedding. Small, pale
green flowers, clustered on long stems growing from
axils of new leaves, are borne in spring after the
tree is in full foliage. The natural range of this tree
includes most of the U.S. east of the Mississippi
River. FLORIDA HABITAT: Cypress swamps and deciduous hardwood swamp forests.

SOUTHERN WAX MYRTLE   *Myrica cerifera*

NATIVE: Southeastern United States.
FAMILY: Myricaceae.   ZONES: N, C, S

Also called Bayberry Tree. This hardy evergreen
tree grows 15–25 feet in height with multiple, lean-
ing trunks up to 1 foot in diameter. Its slender,
spreading branches form a round, narrow crown.
Smooth silver-gray bark is marked with small
splotches. Leaves, aromatic when crushed, are
simple, leathery, bright green with tiny orange spots
on undersides; they are about 4 inches long and 2
inches wide. Yellowish-green flower catkins are
borne in spring, the male and female blossoms on
separate trees. Clusters of small, bluish-gray, wax-
coated berries form along twigs in winter, the "bayberry" used for fragrant candles. Southern Wax
Myrtle grows all over Florida, as it is not harmed
by frost. Although it thrives in moist wetlands, it
does quite well in dry areas and is even tolerant of
sea spray. Limbs are susceptible to wind damage.
FLORIDA HABITAT: Pine flatwoods, cypress swamps,
hydric hammocks.

PIGNUT HICKORY
Carya glabra

NATIVE: Eastern United States.
FAMILY: Juglandaceae.
ZONES: N, C, S

This large deciduous tree has lovely golden leaves in fall and its nuts provide food for squirrels, jays, ducks, woodpeckers, and other birds. It attains a height of 80–100 feet, with its longest and heaviest branches growing near the top of the tree, creating an irregular crown. Its trunk may be up to 2 feet thick and is covered with smooth, thin, gray bark; its surface is broken into crisscrossing ridges, a common trait of hickories.

Leaves are alternate, up to 12 inches long; each has 3–7 dark green, lance-shaped, serrated leaflets 5–7 inches long, arranged opposite each other along the leafstem. Male and female flower catkins are produced on the same tree, in spring. Clusters of pear-shaped nuts mature in fall, each nut enclosed in a thin, ridged husk. The sweet kernels are edible. Pignut Hickory is very drought tolerant, but not salt resistant, and will tolerate periodic flooding. It makes a lovely shade tree or avenue planting. It is best suited to north and central Florida, but will also grow in the upper portion of south Florida. FLORIDA HABITAT: Upland mixed and hardwood forests, hydric hammocks, scrub forests.

WATER HICKORY
Carya aquatica

NATIVE: Eastern United States.
FAMILY: Juglandaceae.
ZONES: N, C

This water-loving tree reaches a height of about 60 feet, with tall, straight trunks 1½–2 feet thick. It has a high, narrow crown of short branches, and bark that is grayish-brown and flaky. Glossy green, feathery leaves have 9–15 leaflets, arranged opposite along a common stem with the odd leaflet at the tip; they are dull green below, with small hairs along the veins. Greenish flower catkins are borne in spring. Bitter nuts grow in clusters of two or more; their thin, 4-ridged husks are round with pointed tips, about an inch wide and 1½ inches long. Water Hickory is deciduous and grows quite slowly. It is a nice choice for shade alongside a pond or stream. Though not tolerant of drought or salt, it is very hardy to cold. FLORIDA HABITAT: Wetland and cypress swamp forests.

SCRUB HICKORY
Carya floridana

NATIVE: Florida.
FAMILY: Juglandaceae.
ZONES: N, C, S

As is the case with many scrub plants, this hickory is smaller than its close relatives that live in more favorable habitats. A slow grower, it may reach a height of 40 feet but is usually smaller. Smooth, greenish-gray bark has tiny, interlacing ridges. Alternate leaves are yellowish-green above, reddish-brown below, 3–4 inches long; 3–7 hairy leaflets grow opposite each other on the stem, with the odd leaflet at the tip. Male and female flower catkins are produced on the same tree, in spring. Round or pear-shaped nuts have thick husks and sweet kernels; they mature in fall and are a valuable wildlife food. Because it is well adapted to very dry, sandy regions, Scrub Hickory is an excellent choice for low water landscapes in areas with poor soil. It is deciduous, requires little or no fertilization and is moderately salt tolerant. FLORIDA HABITAT: Central Florida scrub forests.

CAMPHOR TREE   *Cinnamomum camphora*

EXOTIC: China and Japan.
FAMILY: Lauraceae.   ZONES: C, S

The Camphor Tree is a handsome evergreen often growing to a height of 50–60 feet, its smooth, spreading branches forming a dense, rounded crown. Shield-shaped leaves are aromatic, bright glossy green with prominent, triple, vertical veins; they turn yellow and crimson, shedding just as new young leaves unfold, displaying the soft beauty of their rose-pink coloring. Inconspicuous flowers are dull yellow color and formed in a loose cluster. Flowers are petalless, with several male stamens arranged in series around a single pistil. Small, round, black, pea-like, fleshy fruits have single seeds and are borne in abundance; they hang on the tree long after maturing. Because the seeds are spread widely by birds and sprout readily, Camphor Tree is often guilty of crowding out native vegetation. Valued for the open shade it produces, it is fairly drought tolerant but not salt tolerant nor cold hardy.

RED BAY   *Persea borbonia*

NATIVE: Eastern United States.
FAMILY: Lauraceae.   ZONES: N, C, S

The aromatic leaves of this large evergreen tree are used as a flavoring in cooking. They are also favored by the caterpillars of swallowtail butterflies as a larval food. The Red Bay's spreading crown of shiny leaves makes it a good choice for shade. Plus, it is highly drought and salt tolerant; though hardy to frost it will grow as far south as the Florida Keys. It has few pest problems, will grow in either dry and sandy or moist soil. Its bright green leaves are 2–6 inches in length and have pointed tips. Insignificant pale green flowers appear in spring. Fall brings clusters of bluish-black, ½-inch long berries, a favorite food of birds. Other members of this genus: P. humilis, called Silk Bay for the fine hairs on the underside of its leaves, is a dwarf tree or shrub found in scrub habitat; P. palustris, or Swamp Bay, grows in wetland forests; P. americana is the well-known Avocado. FLORIDA HABITAT: Maritime and upland mesic hardwood forests.

CHERRY-LAUREL   *Prunus caroliniana*

NATIVE: Southeastern United States.
FAMILY: Rosaceae.   ZONES: N, C

Despite its common name, this evergreen tree is not actually a member of the Laurel family. Its supple, shiny, dark green leaves may have finely serrated edges and are poisonous to people and to livestock. It reaches 35–40 feet in height and grows moderately fast. Fragrant white flowers are borne in spring; individually they are insignificant, but the fuzzy-looking clusters are quite attractive. Round, black fruit is a valuable food source for wildlife. Cherry-Laurel is moderately drought tolerant but not salt tolerant. It prefers rich, well-drained soil in full or partial sun. It is very cold hardy, growing throughout northern and central Florida as far south as Lake Okeechobee. Its relatives include peaches and plums. Though not widely used as a landscape subject in the past, it is now available in native nurseries. FLORIDA HABITAT: Upland mesic hardwood forests and scrub forests.

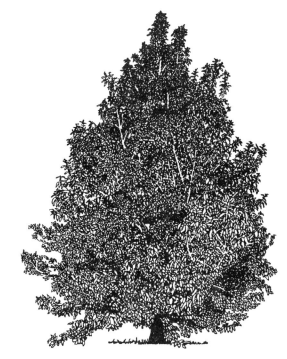

AMERICAN HOLLY   *Ilex opaca*

NATIVE: Eastern United States.
FAMILY: Aquifoliaceae.   ZONES: N, C

Probably the handsomest of all the hollies, this one is found from Massachusetts to Texas and southward to central Florida. Growing to a height of 40–50 feet, it has many short, slender branches that form a dense, conical crown. The bark is light grayish-green. Thick, stiff, leathery leaves are dark, glossy green, 2½–4 inches long; they are slightly curved, with 8–12 shallow lobes forming sharp, marginal spines. American Holly is evergreen, its leaves persisting up to three years before finally shedding. Small, creamy-white or white flowers are borne in midsummer in axils of leaves. On female trees, these are followed by bright red berries which ripen in late fall and remain on the tree until early spring; a male tree also is needed to produce fruit. So extensively has it been harvested for holiday decorations that American Holly has disappeared in many areas and is now protected by law. FLORIDA HABITAT: Upland mesic hardwood forests, and coastal upland forests.

DAHOON HOLLY   *Ilex cassine*

NATIVE: Southeastern United States.
FAMILY: Aquifoliaceae.   ZONES: N, C, S

This handsome evergreen tree grows to 35 feet in height. It has smooth gray bark and is distinctly tree-like. Though its elliptical leaves may be very slightly dentate, they lack the characteristic "holly" shape. However, Dahoon Holly does have beautiful, shiny red berries in fall and winter. Like all hollies, it is dioecious, requiring male and female plants for fruiting to take place. Both male and female trees have small, white, four-petalled flowers that grow along the branches. Though it is native to wet areas, it is very drought tolerant; it is also somewhat resistant to salt, and requires full sun and acid soil. It will grow in both well- and poorly-drained locations. FLORIDA HABITAT: Swamp forests and pine flatwoods.

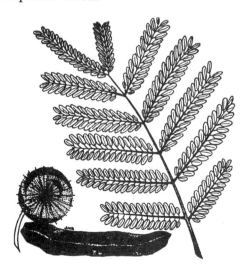

WOMAN'S TONGUE   *Albizzia lebbek*

EXOTIC: Tropical Asia.
FAMILY: Leguminosae.   ZONES: S

This rapid-growing tropical tree has spreading, brittle branches that form an irregular crown. It often attains a height of 50 feet. The comparatively short trunk has smooth grayish-brown bark. Although considered deciduous, its lacy leaves often hang on until new ones begin to grow in spring. The greenish-yellow flowers look like puff balls. They are borne in great profusion and are followed by yellowish-brown seed pods up to a foot long. When the pods become dry, they produce an incessant rattle in the slightest breeze. It is from this characteristic that some wag has dubbed the tree "Woman's Tongue". Once planted for shade, this tree is no longer held in favor; it is messy, always dropping debris, and its weak wood makes it susceptible to wind damage. It can become invasive, prompting some homeowners to remove it.

EARLEAF ACACIA   *Acacia auriculiformis*

EXOTIC: Australia.
FAMILY: Leguminosae.   ZONES: N, C, S

Also called Ear Tree. This fast-growing evergreen reaches 30–40 feet in height, its slender branches forming a dense, wide crown. Long popular for street planting and as a garden specimen, this tree has lost favor in recent years because of its brittle wood and because it constantly drops leaves and pods. Short spikes of yellow flower-catkins are borne in multiples of 2 or 3, followed by coiled pods up to 4 inches long. Flat black seeds are fastened to the pod by yellowish filaments. Pods are shaped like human ears and give this tree its name. Seeds germinate quickly if planted soon after ripening. Earleaf Acacia can also be propagated from cuttings of half-ripened wood.

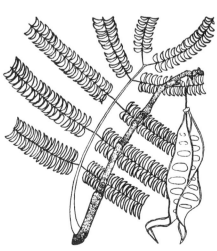

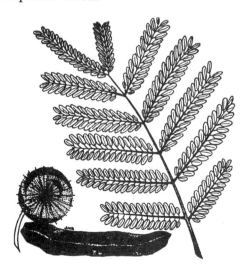

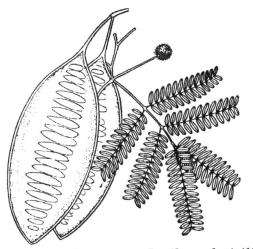

WILD TAMARIND — *Lysiloma latisiliqua*

NATIVE: South Florida and Caribbean.
FAMILY: Leguminosae.　　　ZONES: S

Also called Bahama Lysiloma. This large evergreen tree grows to 50 feet. It has a thick trunk and a wide, flat crown of spreading branches. Feathery leaves are deep green with lighter undersides, similar to those of a true Tamarind. Small, brush-like flowers are greenish-white with pale purple bases. Heavily scented, they appear sporadically throughout the year, but are greatest in number in spring and summer. Broad, flat seed pods are 5 inches long, taper to a point at each end, and have many long, thin, brown seeds. Unlike a true Tamarind (*Tamarindus indica*) it does not have edible fruit. It is highly drought and salt tolerant. Because it is tender to cold and requires well-drained alkaline soil, its natural range is limited to the southernmost part of the state. FLORIDA HABITAT: South Florida rocklands.

SOURWOOD — *Oxydendrum arboreum*

NATIVE: Eastern United States to central Florida.
FAMILY: Ericaceae.　　　ZONES: N, C.

Also called Sorrel Tree, this cold hardy deciduous tree has a slender trunk with coarsely fissured bark and slim, upright branches supporting a loose pyramidal crown. Long, slender leaves are prominently veined, bright glossy green above and lighter beneath, with sharp-toothed margins. Leaves turn bright scarlet in fall before shedding. Conspicuous clusters of small white flowers resembling Lily-of-the-Valley blooms are borne in summer at tips of branches and are followed by grayish, capsular seed pods. Some people consider Sourwood blossom honey to be the very finest. Sourwood is a slow-growing tree that reaches 40 feet. It may be planted as a foreground for larger trees or as a background for shrubbery. It is not salt tolerant, but moderately drought tolerant and may be propagated by seed. FLORIDA HABITAT: Hardwood forests of north Florida, along streams and hillsides where an acid soil is prevalent.

JAMAICA DOGWOOD — *Piscidia piscipula*

NATIVE: South Florida.
FAMILY: Leguminosae.　　　ZONES: S

Also called Florida Fishpoison Tree. This unusual tree grows to 50 feet in height, with an irregularly rounded crown of upright branches and scaly grayish-olive bark. Compound leaves are made up of 7–9 rounded, leathery, dark green leaflets. The leaf veins are usually outlined with reddish-brown fuzz. New leaves are wine-colored. Clusters of purplish-white, sweet pea-like flowers about 3/4 inch long are borne in spring, preceding the leaves. The tree's alternate common name is derived from this poisonous trait: any part of the tree, if crushed and dropped in water, will cause nearby fish to become stupefied and float on the surface of the water. FLORIDA HABITAT: Upland maritime forests.

SPANISH STOPPER   *Eugenia foetida*

NATIVE: South Florida, Central America, Caribbean.
FAMILY: Myrtaceae.   ZONES: C, S

Also called Box-Leaf Eugenia. Round, very dark red, 1/4-inch wide berries are a favorite food of birds. Spanish Stopper will reach up to about 15 feet tall, and may be shrubby or tree-like, depending on its environment. It's evergreen and provides good wildlife cover in the home landscape. It has been used successfully in hedges, as it tolerates severe pruning or shearing. Its dull green leaves are aromatic, oval and pointed at the base, with tiny, dark specks on the undersides. Cream-colored flowers are insignificant, grow in clusters along each branch.

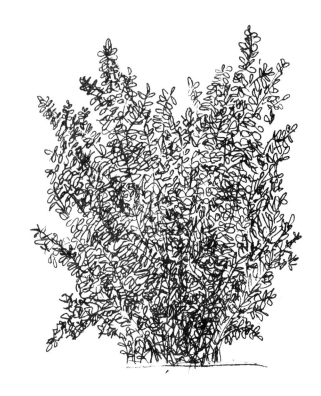

Tiny, round fruit changes from green to red to black as it ripens. Other species available in nurseries: *E. axillaris* (White Stopper), *E. confusa* (Red-Berry Stopper–threatened) and *E. rhombea* (Red Stopper or Spicewood–endangered). Surinam Cherry (*E. uniflora*) is another member of this populous genus; it is non-native and can be invasive. FLORIDA HABITAT: Rockland hammocks and maritime forests.

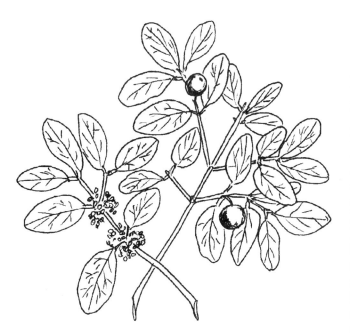

BLACK IRONWOOD   *Krugiodendrum ferreum*

NATIVE: Southeastern Florida and Florida Keys.
FAMILY: Rhamnaceae.   ZONES: C, S

Also called Leadwood, for its extremely dense wood, the heaviest of any tree in North America. This native evergreen deserves wider cultivation. Slow growing, it reaches a height of 25–30 feet and is found in coastal hammocks. It has rough gray bark and soft, oval, glossy green, opposite leaves; these are pale green tinged with red when they first emerge. Insignificant flowers are greenish-yellow and appear in spring. Edible fruit, sweet and berry-like, is 1/4- to 1/2-inch in diameter and black in color. Black Ironwood naturally assumes a shrubby habit but may be pruned to keep it more treelike. It is extremely drought tolerant and also salt tolerant; seedlings can be found in many native nurseries. Subtropical, it grows in south Florida and coastal central Florida. White Ironwood (*Hypelate trifoliata*), also a Florida native tree, occurs in the same type of habitat and also has very heavy, hard wood; it is not related to Black Ironwood. FLORIDA HABITAT: Rockland hammocks and maritime forests.

SHADBERRY
Amelanchier arborea

NATIVE: Eastern United States.
FAMILY: Rosaceae.
ZONES: N, C

Also called Shadbush, Shadblow, Juneberry, Serviceberry. Seldom exceeding 25 feet in height, with narrow crown and small upright branches, the Shadberry is not confined to the tropics, but grows wild in much of the eastern United States. Leaves are yellowish-green, up to 4 inches long, covered with soft woolly white fuzz when young, later becoming smooth. Flowers are borne in early spring, usually before the leaves, in white clusters. Individual blossoms are about 1 inch in diameter; they have long, drooping petals and grow on short stems. Showy and fragrant, they are short-lived. Small round purple fruits ripen in summer, are very attractive to birds. Several seeds are imbedded in the pulp. FLORIDA HABITAT: Upland mixed forests.

CRABWOOD
Gymnanthes lucida

NATIVE: Florida and Caribbean.
FAMILY: Euphorbiceae.
ZONES: C, S

Also called Oysterwood. Drought, salt and wind resistant, this small, slow-growing, evergreen, hardwood tree reaches about 25 feet in height. Its compact crown has shiny, dark green, leathery leaves with prominent veins; they grow to about 3 inches in length. Crabwood blooms in spring, with greenish-yellow male flowerspikes and tiny, red female flowers appearing on the same tree. Fruit is a ½-inch wide capsule that ripens to a very dark reddish-brown, each nut-like fruit suspended on a long stem. Crabwood needs full sun and will grow in almost any soil, provided it has good drainage. It may be damaged by, but will survive, short periods of frost; it may succumb to hard freezes. It may be propagated by seed. FLORIDA HABITAT: South Florida Rocklands.

TOUGH BUMELIA
Bumelia tenax

NATIVE: Southeastern U.S.
FAMILY: Sapotaceae.
ZONES: N, C, S

Also called Tough Buckthorn. Because it is native to coastal areas, this small evergreen tree is extremely salt and drought tolerant. Reddish-brown, fissured bark covers the main trunk; woody stems have small, sharp thorns and green twigs have a downy covering. Leaves are narrowly oblong; they are dark, shiny green above, downy and golden or pale rust-colored below. White flowers are borne in clusters year-round. Black, ½-inch long, egg-shaped fruit is very attractive to birds. FLORIDA HABITAT: Maritime and scrub forests, especially on the east coast and in north central Florida.

GUMBO LIMBO   *Bursera simaruba*

NATIVE: South Florida and Caribbean.
FAMILY: Burseraceae.   ZONES: S

Also called Tourist Tree or West Indian Birch. The Gumbo Limbo's species name comes from its similarity to the Paradise Tree. It has a stout trunk, massive branches, and scaly, reddish bark that is very shiny. It grows 60 feet tall but its weak, porous wood has little value; old-timers used it to make fishing floats. Its leathery leaves, about 3 inches long, are shed in fall. Insignificant, greenish-white flowers are followed by clusters of trian- gular seeds. It was once one of the most common south Florida trees, and many still grow from Cape Canaveral southward on the east coast, and from Bradenton south along the Gulf of Mexico. Gumbo Limbo is tolerant of both drought and salt and is easily propagated by cuttings; even a large limb will grow if stuck into the ground. FLORIDA HABITAT: Rockland hammocks and maritime forests.

PARADISE TREE   *Simarouba glauca*

NATIVE: South Florida and Caribbean.
FAMILY: Simaroubaceae.   ZONES: S

Also called Bitterwood. This slow-growing evergreen reaches nearly 50 feet in height. When young it has an upright form and a smooth brownish-gray trunk; as it ages its crown spreads slightly and the bark develops thick scales. New leaves are reddish, maturing to glossy green with silvery undersides. They are compound, with about a dozen leaflets, each 2–4 inches long; these are arranged alternately along the leafstem, which grows to 8–10 inches in length. Large clusters of tiny, pale yellow or cream-colored flowers are borne in spring. Oval, inch-long fruits are edible but not particularly tasty; their white pulp is an excellent food source for birds. They are green at first, ripening to reddish- or bluish-purple. Paradise Tree adapts to varying soil conditions, preferring a well-drained site in full sun. It is very drought and salt tolerant, and may be propagated by seeds. FLORIDA HABITAT: Maritime forests of both coasts.

44

MANCHINEEL   *Hippomane mancinella*

NATIVE: Tropical America and West Indies.
FAMILY: Euphorbiceae.   ZONES: S

Also called Manzana Apple. This poisonous tropical American tree reaches 20 feet in height. It has a rounded crown, widespread drooping branches, and brown scaly bark with raised lenticels. Rounded leathery leaves on long stems grow to about 4 inches long; polished dark green above, they have lighter undersides and pointed tips. Tiny yellow-green flowers are borne in spring on 6-inch, purplish spikes, with male flowers at the tip, female flowers at the base. Small, toxic, apple-shaped fruits are borne in fall; 1–1½ inches in diameter, they are yellow-green with red cheeks and contain 6 or 8 brown egg-shaped seeds. As do others in its botanical family, Manchineel exudes a milky sap from any injury; highly poisonous and caustic to the skin, it is said to have been used by Caribs for arrow poison. Even moisture dropping from the leaves of this tree is dangerous, and due to its extreme toxicity, it is being destroyed. Once numerous in south Florida, it now is found only occasionally in the Everglades. FLORIDA HABITAT: Estuarine marshes and mangrove hammocks in south Florida.

SAUSAGE TREE   *Kigelia pinnata*

EXOTIC: Africa.
FAMILY: Bignoniaceae.   ZONES: S

Also called Fetish Tree. This tree is grown for its unusual, gourd-like "sausages"; these dangling seed pods may be 2 feet long and 5 inches in diameter. Though inedible, they are used medicinally in some parts of the world; some cultures consider the tree to be sacred. The showy, purplish-red flowers hang like candles on a candelabra, on the ends of cord-like stems that can be 20 feet long. They open at night and last only one night. The tree is evergreen, grows up to 50 feet tall, and tolerates neither salt nor frost. It is fairly drought tolerant. A few are available in nurseries, but the fruits are rather a nuisance and this tree is most often planted as a curiosity in parks or public gardens in south Florida.

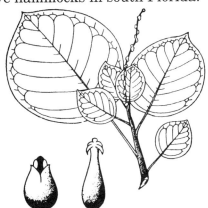

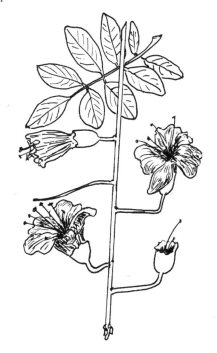

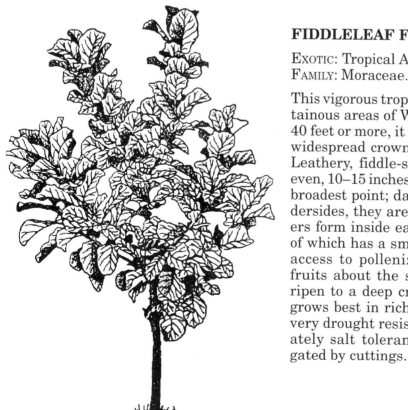

STRANGLER FIG
Ficus aurea

NATIVE: West Indies and South Florida.
FAMILY: Moraceae.   ZONES: S

Also called Golden Fig. Beginning life as an epiphytic climbing vine, it develops aerial roots which eventually become secondary trunks upon reaching the ground, like its relative the Banyan. It reaches heights up to 60 feet, with a broad, rounded crown. Thick, leathery leaves are simple, oval, smooth and glossy dark green above, lighter and downy underneath, 2–4 inches long, narrowing at each end. Flowers are produced continuously inside small, fleshy, globe-like receptacles resembling those of the commercial fig, *F. carica*. Fruits are inedible, red, ³⁄₄ inch long. The name "Strangler" comes from its habit of rooting in and then entwining its host's trunk, while its crown of leaves robs the supporting tree of light. When its roots reach the ground it becomes self-supporting and soon completely smothers its host. It is very drought resistant and somewhat salt tolerant, but can become invasive in the home landscape. FLORIDA HABITAT: Hammocks and wetland forests.

FIDDLELEAF FIG
Ficus lyrata

EXOTIC: Tropical Africa
FAMILY: Moraceae.   ZONES: S

This vigorous tropical shade tree is native to mountainous areas of West Africa. Ranging in height to 40 feet or more, it has a slender trunk and a dense, widespread crown supported by sturdy branches. Leathery, fiddle-shaped leaves are rigid and uneven, 10–15 inches long, almost half as wide at their broadest point; dark glossy green with lighter undersides, they are prominently veined. Tiny flowers form inside each immature fig, the base of which has a small opening that affords access to pollenizing insects. Inedible fruits about the size of a small plum ripen to a deep crimson. Although it grows best in rich, moist soils, it is very drought resistant and moderately salt tolerant. It is propagated by cuttings.

BANYAN

Ficus benghalensis

EXOTIC: East India.
FAMILY: Moraceae.

ZONES: S

Also called Rubber Tree. This tree has been called one of the plant wonders of the world. Its leaves are 6–10 inches long, broadly oval, glossy dark green above, lighter and downy underneath. Round, red fruits ½ inch thick are borne in pairs in summer. The Banyan is easily identified by the many aerial roots that grow from its branches; these develop into trunks when they reach the ground. A single tree, its aerial roots expanding outward, can cover an immense area and may reach a height of over 100 feet. The Banyan is considered to be an exotic pest species in south Florida. Its aggressive root system is also problematic; it can lift or break sidewalks or foundations, and can damage water and sewer systems. Unlike most other drought tolerant trees, it is very fast growing. It is moderately salt tolerant as well.

SCREWPINE

Pandanus veitchii

EXOTIC: Polynesian Islands.
FAMILY: Pandanaceae.

Zones: S

This tropical Old World plant grows 30–40 feet high and has slender, palm-like trunks; these usually are supported by immense prop roots that appear to be lifting the tree from the soil. The common name is derived from the interesting spiral growth habit of the green-and-yellow striped, sword-like leaves, 3 inches across and up to several feet in

length. Small flowers are borne in close spikes or heads. This tree is good for coastal areas as it is tolerant of salt spray. It will withstand drought, but must be protected from frost. Propagation is by seeds or by transplanting the suckers that grow around the base of the plant; remove suckers when very small, using the point of a knife blade. Pot them singly in a sandy loam mixture in small containers, watering sparingly until roots form. Young specimens make excellent house or patio plants. A close relative, *P. utilis*, has large globular fruit with edible meat.

Mangroves

The name "mangrove" refers to the Rhizophoraceae family, with its over 60 species. Florida claims only one of these, the Red Mangrove. But the term mangrove is applied to several other unrelated species that share some common traits: tolerance of salt water and "breather" roots. The Black Mangrove (*Avicennia germinans*), the White Mangrove (*Laguncularia racemosa*) and the Buttonwood (*Conocarpus erectus*) thus qualify as "mangroves".

While only one of these can claim to be a "true" mangrove, all are important in the tidal habitat. The Red Mangrove, with its buttress-like prop roots, has through the centuries served two important functions in Florida where the sea meets the land. One is to protect its shores from the fierce hurricanes that have battered it since time immemorial. Another is to serve as a seaside nursery; a multitude of creatures live and breed within its tangle, impenetrable to many predators. Both above and below the water's surface, the young of birds, fish and even some mammals begin their lives in relative safety.

The Black Mangrove joins the Red in one important function; its above-the-surface roots trap and hold detritus while bacteria digest the fallen leaves and other organic matter, turning it into the nutrients that begin the food chain. The White Mangrove, growing further back, provides a place for roosting shorebirds to nest. Buttonwood, while it tolerates brackish water, grows on high ground as well. It is a favored host for epiphytic plant life.

RED MANGROVE   *Rhizophora mangle*

NATIVE: Tropical America.
FAMILY: Rhizophoraceae   ZONES: C, S

Growing in salt water and reaching a height of 40 feet, the Red Mangrove has been called "walking tree" because its arching proproots continually extend the range of its woody web. Glossy green, leathery leaves are 2–6 inches long and half as wide. Yellow flowers, most numerous in spring, precede berries that are eaten by birds, squirrels and other wildlife. The berry gets a head start on becoming a tree: it develops into an elongated, 6–12 inch shoot called a propagule while still attached to the parent. This shoot is primed and ready, beginning growth almost immediately when it falls into the water below—or drifts away for a more distant toehold to start a new forest. Although Red Mangrove thrives in salt water, it can also live in brackish or even fresh water. It may be that it is predominant near salt water only because it has little competition, since most plants cannot survive there. In fresh water habitats, Red Mangrove is likely to be crowded out by other trees. FLORIDA HABITAT: Mangrove swamps.

BLACK MANGROVE   *Avicennia germinans*

NATIVE: Tropical America.
FAMILY: Avicenniaceae.   ZONES: N, C, S

Smaller than the Red Mangrove, the Black Mangrove is usually no more than 25 feet tall. It also withstands salt water, but its habitat is usually muck or brackish water in the zone between dry land and lapping waves. It is able to take the water it needs and extract the excess salt through its leaves; you can see—and taste—the salt crystals that accumulate there. Blooms are white; the deep green, elliptical leaves continually drop and are replaced throughout the year. It sends out underground (or underwater) horizontal roots that produce pneumatophores. These porous, pencil-thin breathing tubes rise several inches above the muck to supply air, like a snorkel, to the roots below. The color of the bark accounts for Black Mangrove's common name. It is the most cold hardy of Florida's "mangrove" trees. FLORIDA HABITAT: Mangrove swamps.

BUTTONWOOD   *Conocarpus erectus*

NATIVE: Tropical America and West Africa.
FAMILY: Combretaceae.   ZONES: C, S

Also called Button Mangrove. This evergreen tropical and subtropical tree is commonly found along shores and salt marsh areas in south Florida, extending to the Florida Keys. Very tolerant of salt, it also grows inland. Though shrubby in form, it often attains a height of 35–40 feet. Its tall, straight, thick trunks grow in crowded clumps, their dark brown bark irregularly furrowed with flaky ridges. Small lance-shaped leaves are grayish-green or silvery. Tiny, pale purple flowers grow in ball-like clusters about ½ inch wide and 2 inches long; grouped in panicles 6–7 inches long, they are borne throughout the year. Ball-shaped, reddish-brown seed cones have been likened to old-fashioned shoe buttons. In pioneer times, the wood was used for charcoal; early settlers used it extensively for fuel because it gives off very little smoke while burning. Buttonwood is easily propagated from cuttings or from seed, and many nurseries now stock it for use as a shade tree. FLORIDA HABITAT: Coastal marine and estuarine shores and marshes.

WHITE MANGROVE   *Laguncularia racemosa*

NATIVE: South Florida and Caribbean.
FAMILY: Combretaceae.   ZONES: C, S

The White Mangrove may be identified by its foliage, which is lighter green than the other mangroves. It also grows farther inland. It sometimes, but not always, develops pneumatophores, and like the Black Mangrove, excretes excess salt through the pores of its leaves. It is evergreen, with bluntly oval, thick, leathery leaves that are 1–3 inches long. Its tiny, downy, greenish-white, fragrant flowers appear in late spring and early summer. Fruit is green with a tinge of red and holds dark red seeds. Like the seeds of the Black and White Mangroves, these germinate while attached to the tree, and are very small, only about ½ inch in length. FLORIDA HABITAT: Mangrove swamps.

Exotic Pest Trees

Florida's temperate climate is a boon to gardeners, allowing them to grow many interesting plants from around the world. Unfortunately, some "immigrant" plants have found Florida, especially central and south Florida, a little too much to their liking. The warm climate and absence of natural predators and diseases allow their populations to explode. They spread rapidly, pushing out native plants — and the ecosystems that depend on them. The problem is especially acute in Florida because its burgeoning human population also puts pressure on ecosystems. If you care about environmental conservation, do not plant these trees, and if you have one or more of them on your property, consider removing them.

BRAZILIAN PEPPER *Schinus terebinthifolius*

EXOTIC: Brazil.
FAMILY: Anacardiaceae.   ZONES: C, S

Also called Florida Holly and Christmas Berry. This subtropical evergreen tree grows to a height of 20 feet and is found throughout central and south Florida. Its wide, unevenly rounded crown is composed of slender, brittle, upright and spreading branches on a short trunk. Leaves are composed of 5 or 7 leaflets arranged opposite on a common stem, the odd leaflet at the tip. Narrow, satiny-smooth leaflets are dark green with lighter undersides, 1–3 inches long, with prominent veins. They exude an acrid or caustic aroma when crushed. Inconspicuous yellowish-white flowers are borne in clusters in summer, male and female blossoms on different plants. These are followed in winter by clusters of bright red, long-lasting, aromatic berries on female trees. Birds relish the berries and propagate seeds widely. As a result, Brazilian Pepper is rapidly replacing beneficial native species and wiping out ecosystems. Most municipalities prohibit planting Brazilian Pepper and have ongoing programs to remove it from publicly owned property.

MELALEUCA *Melaleuca quinquenervia*

EXOTIC: Australia.
FAMILY: Myrtaceae.   ZONES: C, S

Also called Punk Tree or Cajeput. The tall, shaggy trunk of this tree has thick, brownish-white, spongy bark and heavy, upright trunks. Leathery, gray-green leaves, 3–6 inches long, are slightly aromatic. Though petalless, its flowers are showy, their stamens forming creamy-white spikes that resemble a bottle brush. (Melaleuca is closely related to the Bottle-Brush tree, *Callistemon spp.*, with its showy red or yellow stamens.) Flowers are replaced by closely-spaced, cuplike pods that cover the stem and are filled with tiny seeds. This stem continues to grow at its tip, bearing new leaves and additional branching flower spikes. Melaleuca has become a major nuisance in south Florida, especially in the Everglades. Much time and money has been spent in eradication attempts. Use of its wood as a landscape mulch is highly recommended; this reduces pressure on cypress stands, gets rid of Melaleuca trees, and doesn't contribute on the already overburdened solid waste stream. Most Florida municipalities prohibit the planting of Melaleuca trees.

AUSTRALIAN PINE   *Casuarina equisetifolia*

EXOTIC: Australia.
FAMILY: Casuarinaceae.   ZONES: C, S

Fast-growing, open and upright-branched, this nuisance tree attains heights of 150 feet, and is similar in appearance to a true pine, though it is not one. Technically, trees in this family have no leaves; gray-green "needles" are actually bunches of hair-like jointed branchlets, 4–8 inches long, growing on slender, spreading branches. The family name Casuarinaceae comes from a fancied resemblance of the needles to the feathers of the Australian cassowary bird. Seed cones are about ½ inch thick and nearly 1 inch long, with flat tips and bases and short stems; they are borne singly along branches in great quantities. This salt-resistant tree has been used along beaches as a windbreak and to discourage beach erosion. However, it is not recommended because it spreads rapidly, replaces native species, and creates very thick stands that can become impenetrable. It has become such a pest that many municipalities have ordinances that prevent it from being planted.

CHINESE TALLOW-TREE   *Sapium sebiferum*

EXOTIC: Asia.
FAMILY: Euphorbiaceae.   ZONES: N, C, S

Also called Popcorn Tree. This deciduous tree was imported over two centuries ago by Benjamin Franklin. In the last 25 years it has become a nuisance, first in Texas and now in Florida. It readily sprouts from seed, replacing native species in cypress hammocks and disrupting ecosystems. Once prized as a residential avenue planting, it is now looked upon with disfavor due to its invasive character. Its attractive, deep-green leaves, broadly oval with sharply pointed tips, are poisonous. Long clusters of tiny yellow flowers grow at the tips of its branches in spring. Seed pods are brown, woody and three-lobed. Tens of thousands of them can be produced by one tree in the fall; they can be very messy when they drop. This tree is used in its native region as a source of tallow for making candles, soaps and oils. It's a tough species; it is very drought tolerant, very cold hardy, somewhat tolerant of salt, withstands periodic flooding and thrives in poor soil. Its malignant proliferation may lead to concentrated efforts to eradicate it.

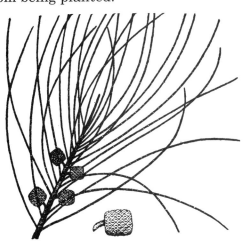

51

UMBRELLA TREE *Schefflera actinophylla*

EXOTIC: Australia.
FAMILY: Araliaceae. ZONES: C, S

Also called Schefflera, Brassia or Octopus Tree. This fast-growing subtropical evergreen tree reaches 30 feet or more in height, its slender trunk encircled almost to the ground by long-stemmed, palmate leaves. The bright green (or variegated green-and-white) compound leaves have an odd number of oval-shaped leaflets; these are arranged rosette fashion at the tip of each stem, like the ribs of an umbrella. Small specimens are common as house plants. When grown outdoors, it produces long, branch-like flower spikes resembling octopus tentacles; these emerge from the very top of the tree in summer, are covered from tip to base with tiny, red flowers and produce many tiny seeds. Commonly grown as far north as Tampa, Umbrella Tree may be killed to the ground by frost but will regrow from the roots. Many cultivars have been developed, including dwarf and variegated forms.

SURINAM CHERRY *Eugenia uniflora*

EXOTIC: Brazil.
FAMILY: Myrtaceae. ZONES: C, S

Most often grown as a pruned hedge, this small tree grows no more than 10–12 feet tall. New leaves are bright, varnish red, maturing to dark glossy green and reaching 2 inches long and an inch wide. Small, single, white flowers are produced in spring. The tasty fruit is an inch wide, deeply ribbed, with glossy, bright red skin and juicy, orange, sweet-tart pulp. There are one or two small round seeds. Fruit is eaten out of hand, or in salads, pies or jellies. It is also relished by birds. Long grown in warm Florida, it has become naturalized and is becoming invasive in some areas. Surinam Cherry is evergreen, tolerates frost, and is moderately resistant to salt and drought.

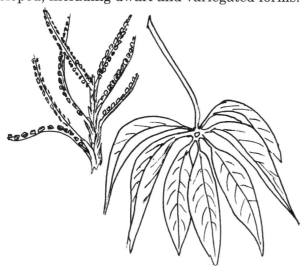

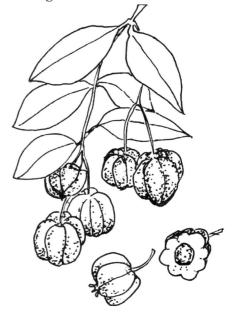

In the sixteenth century a shipload of Spaniards landed on a sandy subtropical beach and announced that the land they had just confiscated would henceforth be called "La Florida." It was not, as is sometimes claimed, because the new peninsula was a "Land of Flowers," but rather because coincidentally, it happened to be the Easter season, called "Feast of Flowers" or "*Pascua Florida*" in Spain.

These newcomers saw a tiny fraction of the flowers that can be glimpsed by a modern visitor, during almost any season, in Florida. This floral abundance is especially noticable in urban areas, where homeowners and landscape artists have developed a varied palette of color for their exterior decorating. Much of this beauty is above our heads, in the trees. Esteemed horticulturist Dr. Edwin Menninger described our flowering trees as Color in the Sky; that was also the title of one of his books on the subject.

South Florida's warm climate has made it a welcoming host to trees native to the tropics. Many of our most colorful botanical immigrants come from Central and South America, Mexico, southern Asia and the Caribbean Islands. Some of these imports have proven to be detrimental, and we wish we had never let them in. However, few among us could look at a purple haze of Jacaranda blossoms on an early spring day, or the shimmering cloud of gold that is a Tabebuia tree in bloom (or at any number of other such splashes of beauty) and ever imagine Florida without them.

Though usually less flashy, native trees provide some beautiful displays as well. Loblolly Bay, Southern Magnolia and Sweet Bay have flowers that are fragrant as well as pretty, and withstand the cold weather that their exotic cousins can't. Lignum Vitae and Geiger Tree are natives that are found nowhere else in the United States. Flowering Dogwood, cherished by many Southerners, provides a showy display in north Florida landscapes. Members of the Hawthorn family are becoming increasing popular as more people opt for landscaping that is a boon to wildlife as well as eye-pleasing.

Profiled on the following pages are just a few of the many flowering trees that may be cultivated in Florida. You might consider choosing several that bloom in different seasons, so that your landscape will have year-round color.

CRAPE MYRTLE   *Lagerstroemia spp.*

EXOTIC: India, Southern Asia.
FAMILY: Lythraceae.   ZONES: N, C, S

There are many cultivars of this fast-growing exotic tree, which reaches 20–35 feet in height, depending on variety. Crape Myrtle is deciduous, its leaves turning red and gradually dropping throughout winter. It has a tendency to become multi-trunked and shrubby, a propensity that may be controlled by severe pruning during its dormant period. Its leaves are obovate, deep green above and light green beneath with faint veining. Summer brings dense, showy racemes of pink, red, lavender or white flowers at the ends of each branch. Migrating warblers relish Crape Myrtle's winged seeds, borne in woody, dark brown, globular seed cases that are about ³/₈ inch wide. Because it withstands extremes of heat and cold, *L. indica* may be cultivated throughout Florida. Its relative *L. speciosa*, Queen's Crape Myrtle, is less cold hardy, thriving only in southern and coastal central Florida. Crape Myrtle is not salt tolerant but is moderately drought resistant.

GOLDEN RAIN TREE *Koelreuteria elegans*

EXOTIC: Japan.
FAMILY: Sapindaceae. ZONES: N, C, S

This flowering tree is attractive summer through winter. In summer, its crown sports upright panicles of showy yellow flowers above the foliage. As they fade, they are followed by salmon-colored seed pods that resemble Japanese paper lanterns. Often a tree has flowers and seed pods present at the same time. The feathery foliage is pretty, too; bright green, compound leaves have 7–15 opposite leaflets. The grayish-brown trunk usually develops several main branches. Golden Rain Tree is often used as a street or shade tree and may grow to 40 feet or more, with an umbrella-like crown that is dense and leafy. Moderately drought and salt resistant as well as cold hardy, it is not particular as to soil type, preferring a well-drained location with lots of light. There are a number of different species of *Koelreuteria*, all of them very similar in appearance.

TRUMPET TREE *Tabebuia spp.*

EXOTIC: Mexico, Central and South America.
FAMILY: Bignoniaceae. ZONES: S

The flowering trees in this genus reach 25-40 feet in height. The different species in cultivation have showy flowers that may be yellow, pink, purple or white: bell-shaped, about 2 inches long, they grow in clusters. Most species are deciduous, their bright blossoms generally appearing just before spring leaves. Silver Trumpet Tree (*T. caraiba*) is named for the silvery undersides of its leaves; it has brilliant yellow flowers, and arguably is the most common *Tabebuia* in Florida. Golden Trumpet Tree (*T. chrysotricha*) is quite large, reaching 40 feet. By contrast *T. umbellata* is smaller, growing to 15 feet; it has fragrant yellow flowers. Purple Tabebuia (*T. impetignosa*), also small, is fairly uncommon in Florida. All are very drought tolerant and moderately salt resistant; they require full sun and periodic fertilization for best flowering and growth. Though subtropical trees, they will withstand short periods of freezing weather; in central Florida they are best situated in coastal areas.

JACARANDA
Jacaranda mimosifolia

EXOTIC: Brazil.
FAMILY: Bignoniaceae. ZONES: C, S

This deciduous tree reaches 40 feet in height and has a slender, pale gray trunk with upright, widely spreading branches. Its finely-cut, fern-like, feathery leaves are 12–18 inches long, with bright green, sharp-pointed leaflets. Loose clusters of large, blue, bell-like flowers (to 2 inches) appear in spring, usually before new leaf growth. Round, flat, woody seed pods are filled with flat, light brown seeds encased in a tissue paper-like covering. Grown as a street tree or yard specimen, especially in southwest Florida, it is drought tolerant but not salt resistant nor especially cold hardy. Some find its shedding leaves, blossoms and seed pods to be messy and a nuisance. Others view a carpet of purple blossoms on their lawn as a thing of beauty.

ROYAL POINCIANA
Delonix regia

EXOTIC: Madagascar.
FAMILY: Leguminosae. ZONES: S

Also called Flame Tree and Flamboyant. This broad-crowned, ornamental, tropical tree may reach 40 feet in height. Its bright green leaves have a feathery softness both in appearance and to the touch. Up to 2 feet in length, they are comprised of 10–20 compound leaflets. Flowers are bright scarlet and orange, 3–4 inches in diameter; they grow in immense clusters and are followed by flat, woody seed pods often 2 feet long. Heavy-trunked older trees are singularly picturesque in the tropical landscape. Somewhat tolerant of salt, they are frequently used as plantings around beach homes. Although it sheds its leaves, Royal Poinciana is barren for only a few weeks in winter. Widely planted in south Florida, it is drought tolerant but susceptible to freeze damage.

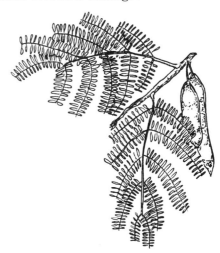

YELLOW POINCIANA *Peltophorum pterocarpum*

EXOTIC: Philippine Islands, Australia.
FAMILY: Leguminosae. ZONES: C, S

Also called Copperpod. This great, umbrella-shaped tree is a relative of the Poinciana; its feathery, compound, deep green leaves are similar. It grows to around 50 feet tall and from May to August displays a golden canopy of blossoms above the crown. Evergreen in warmer areas, it may drop most of its leaves in winter in central Florida; however, its bronzy, winged pods hang on. It is extremely fast growing, and makes a good lawn tree, providing pleasant shade that is not so dense as to prevent the growth of grass or other plants beneath it. It is very drought tolerant and even moderately salt tolerant. The compound leaves are dark green, each made up of hundreds of tiny leaflets. Blossoms are fragrant and are sought by bees.

GOLDEN SHOWER *Cassia fistula*

EXOTIC: India.
FAMILY: Leguminosae. ZONES: C, S

Also called Pudding-Pipe Tree. In Hawaii this tree has adapted particularly well and grows to 50 feet tall, but in Florida it usually reaches no more than 30 feet. Though deciduous, it is rarely leafless. Its spreading, open crown provides abundant shade. Drooping, foot-long clusters of fragrant, golden yellow flowers, 1½–2 inches wide, are borne in late spring; blossoming may continue for several months. Flowers are followed by seed pods up to 2 feet long and 1 inch wide. They can be a nuisance when they fall, littering rooftops and obstructing lawnmowers; when crushed they exude a musky smell. There are over 400 species in the *Cassia* genus, many shrub-like in form, with flowers of varying colors. *C. javanica* has very showy pink and white flowers and is also tree-like. All are tropical. Their foliage provides a larval food for the Orange-Barred Sulphur butterfly. Golden Shower tree is moderately drought tolerant, disdains salt, and can withstand only short periods of freezing temperatures.

PARKINSONIA *Parkinsonia aculeata*

Exotic: Southwestern United States.
Family: Leguminosae. Zones: S

Also called Jerusalem Thorn. Planted extensively in Florida as an ornamental, it attains a height of 25–35 feet. Its slender, greenish-gray trunk is topped by an irregular crown of thorny, willowy, gracefully drooping branches. Tiny, yellowish-green leaves grow on flat leafstems, giving foliage an illusion of delicate lace. Although this tree is deciduous—the leaves are shed very early in spring—the bark of the trunk, the branches and tiny branchlets retain a constant, shimmering greenness. Loose clusters of small, yellow, fragrant, inch-wide flowers are borne in early spring, followed by slender seed pods three to four inches long. This tree is named for the English botanist John Parkinson, who lived from 1567–1650.

ORCHID TREE *Bauhinia variegata*

Exotic: India.
Family: Leguminosae. Zones: C, S

This popular tree is grown extensively in Florida and throughout much of the tropical and subtropical world. *B. variegata* is deciduous, grows to 40 feet, and produces orchid-like, 5-inch flowers in various colors in springtime. At least a half dozen other species of *Bauhinia* trees and shrubs from around the world have been introduced into Florida. A popular one is *B. blakeana*, a 30- to 40-foot evergreen. Its purple "orchids" appear in fall and winter, at the same time the deciduous *B. purpurea*, also purple-flowered, is in bloom. Since *B. punctata*, a red-flowering shrub, blooms in summer and fall, Florida gardens could conceivably have orchid trees flowering all year long. The leaves of all are typically two-lobed. Most are fairly drought tolerant and may withstand some frost. However, none can endure extended low temperatures.

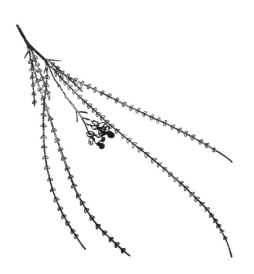

57

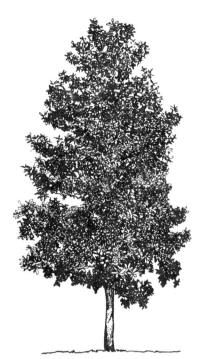

SOUTHERN MAGNOLIA *Magnolia grandiflora*

NATIVE: Southern U.S., southward to central Florida.
FAMILY: Magnoliaceae.   ZONES: N, C

This broad-leaved evergreen reaches 65 feet in height. Its tall, straight trunks grow up to 3 feet thick at the base and have nearly-smooth, grayish-brown bark. Small spreading branches form a dense, symmetric, conical crown. Leathery, glossy-green leaves have downy, grayish-brown undersides, are 5–9 inches long and about a third as wide. They have pointed or rounded tips, wedge-shaped bases, and smooth margins. Many-petalled, creamy-white flowers are 6–8 inches wide and very fragrant; they grow on short, brown, pebbly stems borne at the tips of branches. The cone-like seed pods are themselves very showy. They are 3–4 inches long, with individual seed pockets on the surface that open progressively as the cone ripens, exposing bright red, sweetly aromatic seeds that resemble coffee beans and are good food for woodpeckers and other birds. FLORIDA HABITAT: Upland mesic hardwood and mixed forests, maritime forests, hydric hammocks.

ASHE MAGNOLIA   *Magnolia ashei*

NATIVE: Southeastern United States.
FAMILY: Magnoliaceae.   ZONES: N

This endangered dwarf magnolia reaches only 12–15 feet in height at maturity. Its slender, upright branches form a cone-shaped crown that grows from a small, sturdy trunk 2½–3 inches thick covered by smooth, grayish-brown bark. Its alternate leaves are unusually long, often measuring 20 inches in length; they have a smooth margin with a narrow, inverted-V base. Pale green and glossy above, silvery-gray beneath, they are shed in the fall. In spring, single flowers are borne at the tips of branches as new leaves begin to appear. Flowers are very fragrant, and may be up to 1 foot wide, their long, creamy-white petals arranged around a cone-like center. Long, narrow seed cones mature in summer. Their reddish-brown, egg-shaped seeds are attached to sticky threads that emerge from slits in the surface of the cone. FLORIDA HABITAT: Upland mesic hardwood forests.

SWEET BAY *Magnolia virginiana*

NATIVE: Eastern United States.
FAMILY: Magnoliaceae. ZONES: N, C, S.

Varying from shrub size to 50 feet in height, this tree is evergreen in the south, but deciduous in colder climes. It has an irregularly shaped crown of spreading branches and a tall, straight, thick trunk covered with smooth, light brown bark. Six-inch long, alternate leaves have a leathery texture. They are thin and narrowly oval or boat-shaped, with smooth margins and wedge-shaped tips and bases. Bright green with silvery-gray undersides, they are slightly aromatic. Solitary flowers are very fragrant, borne in late spring at the tips of branches; they are about 3 inches wide with up to 12 short, chalk-white petals. Small seed cones follow in fall, their flat, reddish-black seeds attached by tiny threads released from slits in the surface of the cone. FLORIDA HABITAT: In swamps and along rivers and streams from Massachusetts south to Texas, and south Florida.

TULIP POPLAR *Liriodendron tulipfera*

NATIVE: Eastern United States.
FAMILY: Magnoliaceae. ZONES: N, C

Also called Yellow Poplar. This North American hardwood timber tree grows as tall as 100 feet, its clean, straight trunk reaching 5 feet in diameter. Deciduous, it has broad, bluish-green leaves with indistinct lobes that are abruptly truncated at the tips. The larvae of the Tiger Swallowtail butterfly are especially fond of the leaves. Large, tulip-like flowers are greenish-yellow with orange bases, and are followed by elongated, cone-shaped, inedible fruits. Winged seeds are light brown and boat-shaped. This tree may be propagated from seed or by air layering. Like most members of the Magnolia family, it develops into a handsome specimen ideal for avenue and park planting. The spreading crown of an old tree imparts an aura of tranquil strength. FLORIDA HABITAT: Moist, occasionally flooded hardwood forests.

MAHOE   *Hibiscus tiliaceus*

EXOTIC: Caribbean Islands.
FAMILY: Malvaceae.   ZONES: C, S

Also called Sea Hibiscus. This seashore tree grows
to 40 feet tall and has a shrub-like habit, its numerous, spreading branches forming a broadly
rounded crown. Leaves are leathery, dull dark green
above, lighter and downy beneath, 5–8 inches long.
Nearly round but with a narrow tip and a "V" in its
base, the leaf has a distinct valentine shape. Five-
petalled flowers are borne continuously; they are
about 4 inches wide, yellow with purple centers.
The yellow changes to orange-red later in the day,
then to maroon before the flower falls, so the tree
always presents a variety of colors. Small, silky,
cone-shaped pods contain many brown, kidney-
shaped seeds; they split into five sections when mature. Drought and salt tolerant, and able to withstand the pruning required to keep it hedge-sized,
Mahoe is popular for seaside areas.

FRANGIPANI   *Plumeria spp.*

EXOTIC: Tropical America.
FAMILY: Apocynaceae.   ZONES: C, S

A small deciduous tree, maximum 20 feet in height,
the Frangipani has brittle, spreading, blunt
branches. Leaves, 12–15 inches long, are dark green
with lighter undersides. Lance-shaped and leathery, they are prominently veined, borne in a cluster at the end of each stubby branch. The fragrant
flowers are waxy, with petals lapped "whirlygig"
fashion, and may be creamy white to pale yellow
(*P. alba*) or white, pink or near-red (*P. rubra*). A
snow white hybrid sometimes sold as "Singapore
Frangipani" is more compact and is evergreen in
frost free areas. All varieties are extremely drought
tolerant; a segment of branch, even if allowed to
dry completely, will readily sprout when subjected
to moisture. Frangipani blossoms are made into leis
in Hawaii. In Malaya, where it is popular for cem-
eteries, it is called Graveyard Flower, and in India
it is known as Pagoda Tree or Temple Tree.

LIGNUM VITAE
Guaiacum sanctum

NATIVE: South Florida and Caribbean.
FAMILY: Zygophyllaceae. ZONES: S

The common name of this Florida native means "tree of life"; its resin has been used to treat a variety of different ailments. Its extremely hard wood has been carved into bowling balls, mallets, and other objects. It is one of very few native Florida trees that produces conspicuous blossoms. So few are left in the wild that Lignum Vitae is an endangered species. As it is very slow-growing, it has not become popular as a landscape plant. However, some native nurseries now offer it for sale in frost free areas. Although its natural habitat is in the limestone soils of south Florida, it tolerates a wide range of conditions in cultivation. Evergreen, it reaches 15–20 feet in height, and has a short thick trunk. Its dark green leaflets are smooth and leathery; each is about 1 inch long, and 8–10 of them grow on each compound, pinnate leaf. Rich blue, 5-petalled blossoms are spectacular when the tree is in full bloom; attractive year round, it flowers sporadically. Fleshy orange, capsular fruit pops open when the black, red-jacketed seeds inside it ripen. Because Lignum Vitae is tolerant of both drought and salt and requires little care, more south Florida homeowners should consider including it in their landscape plans. FLORIDA HABITAT: Maritime forest.

GEIGER TREE
Cordia sebestena

NATIVE: Florida Keys and Caribbean Islands.
FAMILY: Boraginaceae. ZONES: S

Also called Geranium Tree and Gerabuyn Tree. Slender and compact, this tree has rough, dark brown bark. Although it usually grows to about 25 feet in height, it sometimes attains a height of 40 feet or more. Grayish-green leaves, 7–8 inches long, have a rough, hairy texture above; they grow in clusters at the tips of branches. Six-petalled, crimped, bell-shaped, orange-and-scarlet flowers are 2 inches wide and are borne in broad terminal clusters. Geiger Tree produces masses of showy blooms in July and August, with a few blossoms appearing sporadically at other times during the year. It is fairly rare in the wild, but a number of nurseries now offer seedlings for sale. Geiger Tree tolerates salt air and considerable drought, but not frost. FLORIDA HABITAT: Lee side of coastal hammocks in the Florida Keys.

ANNATTO
Bixa orellana

EXOTIC: Caribbean and Central America.
FAMILY: Bixaceae.   ZONES: S

Also called Achiote. Often grown as a specimen plant in south Florida, Annatto may take the form of a shrub or a small tree. It reaches 18–25 feet in height, with a bushy crown and a short, slender trunk covered by fibrous bark. Prominently veined leaves are 5–7 inches long, somewhat heart-shaped, with wavy margins and pointed tips. Two-inch wide, white, pink or rose-colored flowers are borne in heavy clusters, followed by spiny, reddish-brown seed pods 1½–2 inches wide. Annatto is cultivated in Mexico and Central America for its seed pods, which have many tiny seeds covered by an orange-red or yellowish substance. This substance contains bixin and orellin, source of a commercially important dye used for coloring butter, cheese and other foodstuffs. Sometimes called Lipstick Tree, Annatto is also planted for its colorful flowers, but not at the beach; it does not tolerate salt and must be protected from wind damage, as well as freezing weather.

LOBLOLLY BAY
Gordonia lasianthus

NATIVE: Southeastern United States.
FAMILY: Theacea.   ZONES: N, C, S

This evergreen tree, a member of the Tea family, is ideal for low-lying areas in the landscape because wet soil or periodic flooding will not hurt it. It is not, however, tolerant of drought or salt spray. Reddish-brown, scaly bark covers its stout trunk and spreading limbs. Its large, white, showy flowers have yellow stamens and strongly resemble Magnolia blossoms. Sweetly fragrant, they appear in late summer or early fall on long stems and may be 2–3 inches in diameter. Seeds are borne in ¾-inch long, hairy, brown, woody capsules. Large, leathery, deep green leaves have serrated edges; they grow up to 6 inches long and turn red before falling. Loblolly Bay attains a height of 30–40 feet and requires rich, moist, acid soil. FLORIDA HABITAT: Hydric hammocks of north and central Florida.

FRINGE TREE · *Chionanthus virginicus*

NATIVE: Eastern United States.
FAMILY: Oleaceae. · ZONES: N, C

This small, slow-growing, deciduous tree reaches approximately 30 feet in height. In spring its branches are covered with great masses of tiny, creamy white, 4-petaled, narrow flowers, the drooping clusters resembling feather boas. These are followed in summer by bluish-black fruit, ½–1 inch long, poisonous to people but relished by wildlife. A member of the olive family, Fringe Tree has long been prized as a landscape subject for its showy, fragrant flowers, adaptability to different habitats, and compact growth habit. It will tolerate short periods of drought but not salt spray and prefers moist, acid, fertile soil in partial to full sun. Pygmy Fringe Tree, *C. pygamae* is a dwarf relative that is also native to Florida; it is endangered. Chinese Fringe Tree, *C. retusa*, is an exotic member of the genus with larger flowers. FLORIDA HABITAT: Upland mesic hardwood forests and hydric hammocks.

BOTTLEBRUSH TREE · *Callistemon spp.*

EXOTIC: Australia.
FAMILY: Myrtaceae. · ZONES: C, S

There are several different species of *Callistemon*, all of them evergreen, 15–20 feet high when mature, and most having red flowers. Actually, the flowers themselves are insignificant, it is the mass of bristly red flower stamens at the terminus of each branchlet that is showy. A relative of the troublesome Melaleuca tree, Bottlebrush has foliage and flowers that are similarly shaped, but it appears not to be invasive. It has dark grayish-brown, deeply-furrowed bark; its trunk and branches are slightly crooked, supporting a broad canopy of narrow, elliptical leaves. *C. viminalis* has a decidedly drooping appearance, while *C. rigidus*, as its name implies, stands more erect. Bottlebrush Trees are moderately drought and salt resistant and will tolerate short periods of frost. They require a location with full sun.

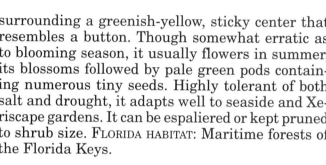

PITCH APPLE   *Clusia rosea*

NATIVE: Florida Keys.
FAMILY: Guttiferea.   ZONES: S

An unusual landscape choice for frost-free areas, this striking evergreen tree is a Florida native, but only in the lower Keys. Its large, leathery, deep green leaves have caused some to call it Autograph Tree; markings scratched on its rubbery leaves remain visible for some time, and people used to plant it in dooryards to serve as a novel "message taker." A small tree reaching 30 feet tall, it may be recognized by its thick dark leaves and colorful blooms. They are 4 inches across, white with a pink ring surrounding a greenish-yellow, sticky center that resembles a button. Though somewhat erratic as to blooming season, it usually flowers in summer, its blossoms followed by pale green pods containing numerous tiny seeds. Highly tolerant of both salt and drought, it adapts well to seaside and Xeriscape gardens. It can be espaliered or kept pruned to shrub size. FLORIDA HABITAT: Maritime forests of the Florida Keys.

FLOWERING DOGWOOD   *Cornus florida*

NATIVE: Eastern United States.
FAMILY: Cornaceae.   ZONES: N, C

The natural range of this tree is from Massachusetts to central Florida. It grows to 25 feet in height, with a broad crown of slender, upright branches. Its comparatively short trunk has dark brown bark that is usually furrowed and flaky on older trees. The *"florida"* in its scientific name means "flowering," not the state of Florida, for this tree is better adapted to areas farther north; it is seldom seen south of Tampa. It requires acid soil and does not tolerate severe drought. Leaves are dark, dull green above, light gray-green underneath, and are shed in fall. Small, pale green flowers are inconspicuous; the showy white "petals" surrounding them are actually bracts. Clusters of small, scarlet, egg-shaped seed pods follow, each pod having a hard, light brown seed embedded in coarse yellow pulp. Flowering Dogwood is easily propagated from mature wood cuttings or by layering. FLORIDA HABITAT: Upland mixed forests.

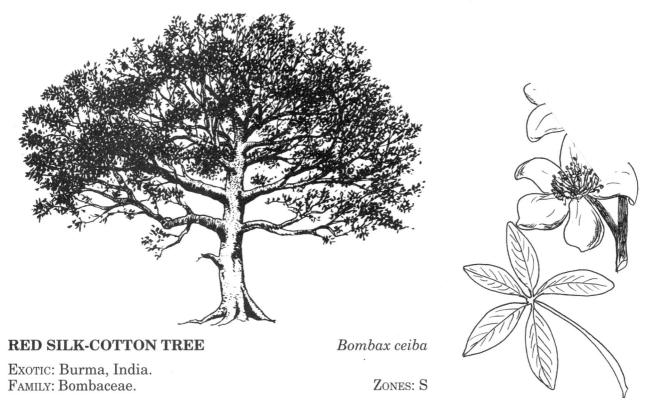

RED SILK-COTTON TREE   *Bombax ceiba*

EXOTIC: Burma, India.
FAMILY: Bombaceae.   ZONES: S

This giant tree is sometimes mistakenly called "Kapok" because it produces floss. Many specimens are found in south Florida, where it was introduced over 100 years ago. The waxy blossoms appear in winter on gray, leafless branches; the bare branches and large red blossoms set against the cloudless blue of a Florida winter sky is a spectacle to behold. Bright crimson, fleshy, 4-inch flowers have stamens almost as long as the petals. Birds and squirrels relish the blossoms, and in some parts of the world, they are also eaten as vegetables by human diners. After the blossoms, woody pods appear which contain silky floss and numerous black seeds.

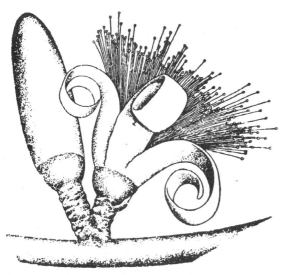

SHAVING-BRUSH TREE   *Pseudobombax ellipticum*

EXOTIC: West Indies, Tropical America.
FAMILY: Bombaceae.   ZONES: S

This is one of the most unusual flowering tropical trees that grow in south Florida gardens. It seldom grows taller than 25 feet. Its wide crown is rarely completely covered with foliage, showing off its attractive green bark. Large, handsome leaves are shaped like the palm of a hand when fully developed; they are purplish-red when they first appear in spring. Leaves begin to fall during the first cool days of winter, with the tree becoming completely bare by early January. Before new spring leaves appear, the bare branches are covered with flower buds 3–4 inches long. They resemble huge elongated acorns, or fat cigars stuck in a cup-like holder. Buds open at night with an explosive sound; as they split, purplish-pink petals curl back to the stem like a cluster of wood shavings, exposing hundreds of long pink, red or white bristle-like stamens, each tipped with golden-yellow pollen. The flowers are followed by a capsular pod containing small seeds embedded in a cottony substance. Shaving-Brush Tree is propagated by cuttings. Although it cannot withstand hard freezes, it is moderately tolerant of both drought and salt air.

FLOSS-SILK TREE *Chorisia speciosa*

EXOTIC: Brazil.
FAMILY: Bombacaceae.   ZONES: S

The most unusual trait of this tropical, deciduous, flowering tree is that the size, shape and color of its flowers vary considerably among individual specimens. The blossoms of a tree grown from seed may look quite different than those of its parent. Flowers are pale to bright pink or violet, with five petals and a very prominent stamen. Leaves are deep green, palmate, with five ovate, serrated leaflets. Floss-Silk Tree grows to about 40 feet, blooms from October to December, and has a greenish-tan trunk completely covered with big, sharp thorns. Like the other members of the Bombax family profiled here, its blossoms appear after the tree has dropped its leaves, which makes its autumn show seem all the more spectacular.

SILK-COTTON TREE *Ceiba pentandra*

EXOTIC: Tropical America.
FAMILY: Bombaceae.   ZONES: S

Also called Kapok Tree. This large tropical tree often attains 100 feet in height in its natural range, its upright branches spreading widely. The thick, sturdy trunks of older trees have surface roots that form buttresses extending several feet. Older trees have thick, warty thorns on their trunks, while younger trees have prickly spines. The large, grayish-green, compound leaves have five leaflets and are shed in late winter. Pinkish-white flowers are borne while the tree is barren of leaves; they are rather small and not particularly attractive. Seed pods mature 2–3 months later. The pods, shaped like a small sweet potato, are light brown, 3–4 inches long and about 1½ inches in diameter; they are filled with small, hard, pea-shaped, cotton-covered seeds. The creamy-white, flossy cotton, or

"kapok" has been used commercially for stuffing pillows and life jackets. Moderately salt resistant and very drought tolerant, this tree is extremely sensitive to frost.

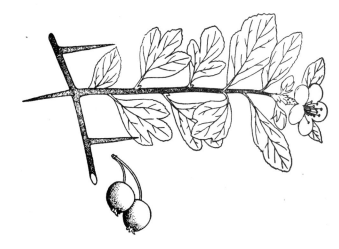

MAY HAWTHORN — *Crataegus aestivalis*

NATIVE: North America.
FAMILY: Rosaceae ZONES: N, C

Also called Shining Hawthorn. Growing to 20 feet with a slender trunk, this tree has grayish, flaky bark and the slender, spiny, crooked twigs typical of the Rose family. Leaves are 1–1½ inches long, glossy with grayish undersides, and are shed in fall. Flowers, ½ inch wide with 5 white petals and pink stamens, grow in clusters. These are followed by round, reddish-orange, edible fruits. Each is about ½ inch in diameter, and has 5 capsule-shaped seeds. May Hawthorn is planted more as a flowering shrub than for its fruit, which attracts birds and other wildlife. FLORIDA HABITAT: Hydric hammocks.

PARSLEY HAWTHORN — *Crataegus marshalli*

NATIVE: Eastern United States.
FAMILY: Rosaceae. ZONES: N, C

This small tree grows only 15–18 feet high. Its slender, often crooked, trunk is grayish-brown; smooth, flaky outer bark exposes patches of lighter-colored bark beneath. The loose, irregular crown has small, angular branches and twigs with slender spines. Leaves, glossy green with lighter undersides, up to 1½ inches long, are shed in winter. Lobed and serrated, they resemble the leaves of cilantro or parsley. Tiny flowers are only ½ inch wide, with 5 white petals and pinkish stamens; they are borne in clusters on short hairy stems. Edible fruit ripens in late summer; it is about ½ inch long with bright yellow skin and yellow flesh. Parsley Hawthorn's interesting foliage and delicate flowers have made it a popular landscape choice among native plant enthusiasts. FLORIDA HABITAT: Hydric hammocks.

SUMMER HAWTHORN — *Crataegus michauxii*

NATIVE: Southeastern United States.
FAMILY: Rosaceae. ZONES: N, C

Also called Yellow Hawthorn. The Florida Association of Native Nurseries calls this small tree an "exceptional plant" for Xeriscapes. Recommended for patios and small yards, it reaches a height of about 15 feet. Like the other hawthorns, it is deciduous and has spiny branches. Its white, 5-petalled flowers are fragrant, about ½ inch long when fully open. Pretty but inedible fruit is golden yellow with a blush of red, about ¾ inch long. Soft leaves are bright green, obovate with serrated edges, growing to about 2 inches in length. Summer Hawthorn needs well-drained, sandy soil, preferably in full sun. A slow-growing tree, it is extremely drought tolerant and very cold hardy, but not resistant to salt. FLORIDA HABITAT: Scrub forest.

Florida—especially south Florida—is home to many fruit trees that won't grow anywhere else in the continental U.S. Quite a few are exotic, but some are native. Citrus, which most people wouldn't consider extraordinary, *is* nevertheless an exotic. Even though oranges and grapefruit are as familiar as bread or milk in every state in the nation, a visitor to the Sunshine State will find in backyards a wide array of citrus varieties that he never met in the supermarket; he has likely known only those that ship well.

Where backyard fruit is concerned, citrus trees are only the beginning. Our "exotic fruits" are myriad. Mango, Jaboticaba, Lychee, Avocado, Carambola, Loquat and a host of others are cultivated, mostly in backyards or as landscape subjects. And these are just the ones we plant and tend. Additionally, any latter-day Euell Gibbons will find that Florida's swamps and forests will yield abundant wild fruits and other foods for the "stalking," if he knows where to look. (A number of books have been published about Florida's wild edibles. Authors Dick Deuerling and Marian Van Atta come to mind.) *Bon appetit!*

Citrus

The Rue or Citrus family — herbs, shrubs and trees native to tropical and subtropical regions — is comprised of some 100 genera and nearly 800 species. Frequently evergreen and mostly woody, most of the genera are glandular and strong-scented. The Rue family is best known for citrus fruits, which today comprise a major fruit crop in the Western Hemisphere. Many "new" citrus fruits have been developed through hybridization. For instance, when Grapefruit (itself a hybrid) was crossed with the Mandarin (Tangerine or Satsuma) we called the resulting fruit Tangelo. A cross between Mandarin and Sweet Orange produced Tangar. There are others, and no doubt more to come. The Sour Orange, *Citrus aurantium*, has played an important role as one of the rootstocks on which is grafted the many varieties of citrus that we enjoy. Which rootstock to use for what, and where to use it, is a science in itself and a subject of great interest to the citrus industry.

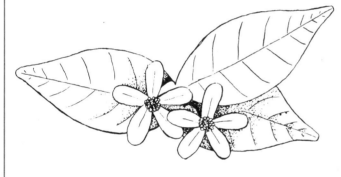

GRAPEFRUIT *Citrus paradisi*

EXOTIC: West Indian hybrid.
FAMILY: Rutaceae. ZONES: C, S

The grapefruit was introduced in Florida in the early 19th century. It is evergreen, grows 30–40 feet tall, with spreading branches on a stocky trunk. Leathery, dark green leaves are 3–6 inches long. Clusters of fragrant, waxy white blossoms an inch wide appear in late winter or early spring. The yellow fruit grows in great, grape-like clusters and has a very juicy pulp that may be yellow, pink or reddish, depending on the variety. Grapefruit trees are hardy throughout central Florida. South Texas and California are the only other areas of the United States with climates suitable for widespread commercial production. Some of the best-known varieties are: Duncan, Marsh, Thompson, Hall, Ruby Red and Foster.

SWEET ORANGE
Citrus sinensis

EXOTIC: China (hybrid)
FAMILY: Rutaceae.   ZONES: C, S

Many people have never seen an orange tree, but most have tasted its fruit. The sour orange was introduced by early Spaniards and for a long time it was propagated only by seeds, resulting in almost endless and unpredictable variety. Today's sweet orange is the product of years of cross breeding for the most desirable qualities, and trees are propagated by grafting or "budding". Today's Sweet Orange tree is evergreen, seldom exceeds 30 feet in height, is heavily branched with a rounded crown and smooth, grayish-green bark. It is usually thornless. Floridians have honored the sweetly fragrant, white, waxy blossom by choosing it as the state flower. Bees appreciate citrus blossoms too, producing commercially sold orange blossom honey. Some beekeepers from northern states go so far as to truck their hives south so that their bees can gather citrus pollen. Commercial citrus growers choose varieties for fruit that ships well, produces high juice yield, are disease resistant, or for other reasons. Backyard growers do not have the same restrictions and have many varieties from which to choose. Since some ripen early, others midseason, and still others late, it is possible to have ripe fruit throughout many months.

CALAMONDIN ORANGE
Citrofortunella mitis

EXOTIC: Philippines.
FAMILY: Rutaceae.   ZONES: S

Usually only 10–12 feet tall, this small evergreen is grown mainly as an ornamental. The glossy, dark green leaves, 1½–3 inches long, are aromatic when crushed. With its rounded crown and fragrant, chalky white flowers, it makes a handsome addition to the landscape. Also, it is nearly everbearing. The small, round, waxy, orange-colored fruit is a bonus. The orange pulp is juicy, very acid, and makes tasty marmalade. It is widely planted in Hawaii and many other subtropical areas.

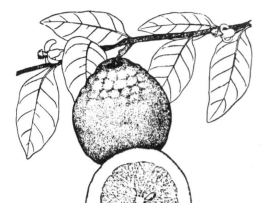

LEMON
Citrus limon

EXOTIC: Asia and India.
FAMILY: Rutaceae.
ZONES: C, S

The lemon is grown in most warm climates of the world. An attractive tree in the landscape, its fruit is a welcome plus. An irregular crown of thorny branches and leathery evergreen leaves are a backdrop for fragrant white flowers. Lemon trees grow to about 15 feet and have a short trunk 3–5 inches in diameter, with a relatively smooth, greenish-brown bark. Meyer lemons are of good quality and several cultivars are available from nurseries. The fruit is less sour than the Ponderosa, and is said to be an orange-lemon cross. The large, up to 7-inch long, Ponderosa Lemon (pictured at left) is warty skinned and its juice is very sour. While considered inferior by some, many people prize it for its thick rind, which they use to make candied peel.

PERSIAN LIME
Citrus latifolia

EXOTIC: Southern Asia.
FAMILY: Rutaceae.
ZONES: S

This small citrus tree reaches 10–15 feet in height. Its irregular crown of thorny branches surmounts a short, sturdy trunk with pebbly-smooth, greenish-brown bark. Dark, glossy-green leaves are paler underneath, leathery and egg-shaped with finely-notched margins. Fragrant flowers are chalky white, waxy with yellow stamens. Large oval fruit is usually about 3 inches long, with dark green skin and pulp, yellow when ripe, usually seedless. Fruit is harvested while green, the main season being late summer and fall. Grown extensively in warmer areas of the Florida peninsula as a backyard plant and commercially, it is commonly grafted on rough lemon seedling stock.

KUMQUAT
Fortunella japonica

EXOTIC: China.
FAMILY: Rutaceae.
ZONES: N, C, S

This small member of the Citrus family (rarely more than 12 feet tall) is prized as a landscape or patio subject as well as a producer of fruit. There are several varieties, some adapted to cool northern Florida, others better for warmer regions. Your nurseryman can help you choose the one best for your area. Flowers are chalk white, fragrant, and 1/2 inch wide. The round or oval, 1 1/2-inch long fruit is bright, glossy orange when ripe. Its thin, pungent rind, rich in vitamin C, is eaten along with the pulpy fruit, which also makes delicious preserves.

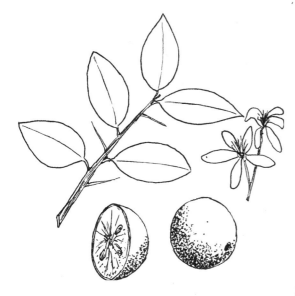

KEY LIME *Citrus aurantifolia*

EXOTIC: Southern Asia.
FAMILY: Rutaceae. ZONES: S

This small evergreeen tree, 10–15 feet in height, has a crown composed of sprawling, thorny branches atop a short, sturdy trunk. Leaves, 1½–3 inches long, are dark, glossy green with pale undersides, leathery and aromatic. The fragrant white flowers are waxy. Fruit is small, thin-skinned and turns yellow when ripe. Key Lime is grown extensively as a dooryard plant in frost free areas. Though originally from another continent, Key Limes became an important commercial crop for Florida Keys dwellers nearly a century ago. They used them to make the now well-known Key Lime Pie. In it, they used canned milk, which was more readily available than fresh milk before bridges joined the Keys to peninsular Florida.

Other Fruit Trees

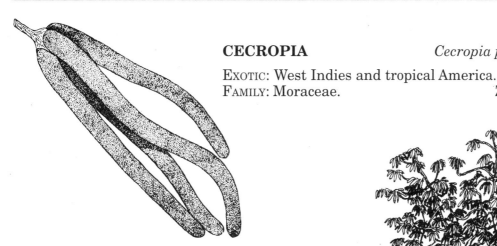

CECROPIA *Cecropia palmata*

EXOTIC: West Indies and tropical America.
FAMILY: Moraceae. ZONES: S

Also called Snakewood. This fast-growing tree may reach 40–50 feet in height. Its trunk is slender to medium-sized, of soft wood with a hollow stem; usually it has few branches except in its umbrella-like crown. Large, handsome leaves 8–10 inches long are shaped like the palm of a human hand, with 7–11 deep lobes. They are light green with a light, downy-textured underside. Slender male and female flower catkins are borne on separate trees. Slim, cylindrical fruits grow in clusters, are less than ½ inch thick and 4–6 inches long; they are brown when fully ripe and taste very much like a ripe fig. The Cecropia is found primarily on the southwest coast of Florida, where it is grown as an ornamental. Its dried leaves are highly prized by flower arrangers.

ROSE APPLE
Syzygium jambos

Exotic: East Indies.
Family: Myrtaceae.   Zones: S

This tropical evergreen tree, to 25–30 feet in height, produces showy flowers and edible fruit. Drooping branches and lateral branchlets form a rounded, compact crown. Older trees may become "scraggly" in appearance. Thick, shiny green leaves grow to 8 inches long and 2–3 inches wide. New leaves, glossy pink and red, present a striking appearance. Chalk-white flowers are 1½–2 inches wide; their many slender stamens resemble loose-tufted brushes. Blossoms are borne singly or in small clusters of 2 or 3, on long stems, widely spaced and near the ends of branches. Round, apple-shaped, yellowish-pink fruit is about 2 inches in diameter. It has a distinct rose fragrance and flavor when fully ripened and may be used to make preserves. The hollow center has 2–4 rough, brown seeds. Grown successfully only in south Florida, it has become a pest.

CHICKASAW PLUM
Prunus angustifolia

Native: Southeastern United States.
Family: Rosaceae.   Zones: N, C

This deciduous American plum is more shrubby than tree-like, reaching 15–20 feet in height. Its slender trunks are 5–8 inches thick and are covered with smooth, blackish-brown bark that sometimes has many fine, crisscrossing furrows. Shiny, bright green leaves are alternate, about 2 inches long and an inch wide at the center, with pointed tips and rounded, wedge-shaped bases. Flowers are borne in early spring before leaves appear; about ⅓ inch wide and chalk-white, they grow in small clusters on slender stems. Round, bright, reddish-yellow fruit about 1 inch thick matures in early summer. The large, solitary seed is encased in a tart, juicy, yellow pulp. Though the fruit is edible (use it to make delicious jelly), the leaves and seeds are poisonous. Florida habitat: Upland mixed forests in north and central Florida.

COCOPLUM   *Chrysobalanus icaco*

NATIVE: South Florida and Caribbean.
FAMILY: Chrysobalanaceae.   ZONES: S

This subtropical evergreen tree reaches 15–20 feet in height. Its dense, broad crown of upright branches tops a trunk 10–12 inches in diameter with reddish-brown flaky bark. Alternate, dark green leaves have a polished, leathery texture; they are 1½–4 inches long. Though some are nearly round, most are slightly heart-shaped at the tip, with a rounded, wedge-shaped base and smooth margins. Clusters of tiny, flat, white flowers are borne year-round, growing on short, creamy-colored stems. Small, round fruit about the size of a half dollar is edible; slightly aromatic, it has purplish skin and thin, white, juicy pulp. The solitary, round seed is nearly as large as the fruit and is an important wildlife food. An attractive landscape plant, Cocoplum is very tolerant of salt and moderately drought resistant. FLORIDA HABITAT: Coastal, upland forests and rockland hammocks.

FLATWOODS PLUM   *Prunus umbellata*

NATIVE: North and Central Florida.
FAMILY: Rosaceae.   ZONES: N, C, S

Also called Hog Plum. This small deciduous tree produces white, showy flowers in early spring before the leaves. It grows to 15–20 feet and has edible fruit, though its leaves and seeds are poisonous. Bright green, simple, alternate, oval leaves have serrated edges and sharply pointed ends. Flowers are about ½ inch wide, with 5 petals; they attract butterflies and bees. Tart red or yellow fruit ripens to a deep purplish-blue color and grows in clusters. Flatwoods Plum is fast growing and somewhat drought tolerant, but does not withstand salt spray or extended periods of flooding. It will grow in full or partial sun and prefers loamy, well-drained soil. FLORIDA HABITAT: Upland mixed and hardwood forests.

PIGEON PLUM   *Coccoloba diversifolia*

NATIVE: South Florida and Caribbean.
FAMILY: Polygonaceae.   ZONES: S

Also called Tie Tongue, for its extremely tart fruit, and Dove Plum. Reaching 35 feet in height, this tree has a 2-foot thick trunk and smooth, grayish-brown, flaky bark which often shows patches of purple. Its leathery leaves are alternate, glossy green above and lighter underneath; prominently veined, they are 3–4 inches long and egg-shaped, with smooth margins. Inconspicuous white flowers are borne in spring on 3-inch long spikes. Purple, plum-like, edible fruit about ½ inch long ripens in late winter and has a single, hard seed. Highly drought and salt tolerant, Pigeon Plum grows best in rich, sandy soil. It may be propagated by seed or from cuttings of ripe wood. FLORIDA HABITAT: Coastal, upland forests and rockland hammocks.

GUAVA · *Psidium guajava*

Exotic: Mexico to Central America.
Family: Myrtaceae.   Zones: S

This 20-foot tree with slender trunk and spreading branches has light brown, scaly bark. Four- to six-inch long leaves are dull green with a downy texture. Creamy-white flowers are about the size of a half dollar and have white and yellow stamens. Round, yellow fruit is 4–5 inches long and has white,

yellow or pink pulp which is strongly aromatic and contains many small, hard seeds. Guavas are grown in south Florida as dooryard plantings, their fruit used to make guava jelly, paste or preserves. The Guava is quite drought tolerant but does not do well near the salty coast. The Cattley or Strawberry Guava (*P. littorale*) is not recommended as a landscape subject; it has naturalized and become invasive in central and south Florida.

MANGO · *Mangifera indica*

Exotic: India, Southern Asia.
Family: Anacardiaceae.   Zones: S

This tropical evergreen tree may reach 75 feet, with an equally wide crown, although grafted varieties grown commercially and for home planting seldom exceed 40–50 feet. The sturdy trunk has many large, lateral branches supporting a well-rounded, dense crown. Mango trees rarely are found north of Tampa. Smooth, glossy green leaves are 6–10 inches long. Flushes of new growth are wine-colored, or occasionally glossy white, red or yellow. Small, cream-colored, fragrant flowers have a reddish tinge; they are borne in clusters on upright spikes from December to April. Mature fruit is pale green to yellow, often flushed with orange or deep crimson. Egg-shaped, it is 3–8 inches long, its flesh fibrous to smooth, very juicy and sweet to mildly acid; some undesirable varieties have a strong turpentine flavor. Each fruit contains one large seed. Mangoes are to the tropics what apples are to temperate regions. Many cultivars are available, most grafted. The Mango is fairly drought tolerant; in fact, it bears best in years when there is little rainfall during its flowering period. It is somewhat salt resistant but will not tolerate extended frost. Other members of this family are Cashew and Pistachio, as well as Sumac and Poison Ivy, which are allergens; Mangoes cause an allergic reaction in some people as well.

SEA GRAPE — *Coccoloba uvifera*

NATIVE: South Florida and Caribbean.
FAMILY: Polygonaceae.   ZONES: S

This multi-trunked, evergreen tree grows to about 20 feet tall. It is picturesque in the landscape and the fruit is a boon to wildlife. The leathery, nearly circular leaves are 6–8 inches wide, dark green above and lighter below, with reddish veins. Clusters of creamy white flowers are borne on thick spikes at leaf axils in late spring. The fruit grows in grape-like clusters, ripens in late summer, and may be pale green to deep purple. It makes tasty jelly and also provides food for wildlife. Salt resistant Sea Grape grows wild along south Florida shores and thus is a good beach garden plant. Its drought tolerance makes it a valuable Xeriscape subject. It may be pruned heavily to desired shape and size; its natural, round, shrub-like form can be maintained, or the lower limbs may be removed to create a canopy of leaves above. Big-Leaf Sea Grape (*C. pubescens*) grows much taller, has huge leaves, and is non-native. FLORIDA HABITAT: Coastal dunes and maritime forest.

AVOCADO — *Persea americana*

EXOTIC: Tropical America.
FAMILY: Lauraceae.   ZONES: S

Grown in Florida since the 1800s (when it was called Alligator Pear), the Avocado has been cultivated in Mexico for centuries. It can stand more drought than cold, thriving only in our frost free or nearly frost free areas. Fast growing and evergreen, it is popular in south Florida as a shade tree. Grafting is a must for fruit production; seeds do not come true. Many varieties are available from nurseries. Trees grow to 40 feet tall, are not choosy as to soil, but do not like salt spray. Supplemental irrigation may be necessary for adequate fruiting. Small greenish-white flowers grow in clusters. Pear-shaped fruit, 7–12 inches long, is picked green when it has reached mature size and allowed to ripen off the tree. Fruit is ripe from June to January, depending on variety. The creamy, butter-like pulp surrounds a single, large, round, brown seed. "California" avocadoes are smaller, have more fat and less moisture than their Florida cousins. They are derived from a different species, *P. drymifolia*.

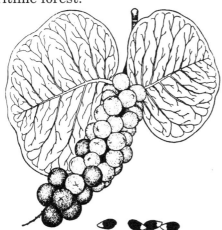

75

CUSTARD APPLE
Annona reticulata

EXOTIC: West Indies.
FAMILY: Annonaceae.
ZONES: S

This small semi-evergreen tree, sometimes called Bullock's Heart, is one of nearly a dozen small fruit trees, closely related and similar in appearance, that have edible fruit and grow in tropical America. The round, 6-petalled flowers of the Custard Apple are tiny and greenish-yellow. Fruits ripen in early spring and weigh about a pound apiece; they are heart-shaped, about 6 inches long, and have yellow or tan skin with a reddish blush. The fruit has a creamy pulp that contains many brown, bean-shaped seeds. Long, pointed, oval leaves grow alternately along the branch and are dark green and leathery. The mildly sweet fruit is almost flavorless, and is best used in custards, ices, or milkshakes. The Custard Apple can withstand drought, but not frost, and is only moderately salt tolerant. The bark is poisonous. Other fruit-bearing members of the Annona genus are the Soursop and Cherimoya. The Pond Apple (below) is also sometimes referred to as Custard Apple.

SUGAR APPLE
Annona squamosa

EXOTIC: West Indies.
FAMILY: Annonaceae.
ZONES: S

Also called Sweetsop. This small tropical tree reaches 10–20 feet in height, its long, slender branches forming a rounded crown. Leaves are thin and narrow, 3–6 inches long, dull green, and are shed in late winter. Yellow flowers have a hint of green; they are borne on short stems in small clusters of 3 or 5. These are followed by heart-shaped, cone-like fruit. The thick, yellowish-green, scaly rind is tinged with a powdery white substance that rubs off when the fruit is handled. Fruit is harvested just before maturity, as it splits if it ripens on the tree. The tree will produce ripe fruit for as much as six months of the year. The sweet, creamy-white pulp has a pleasant flavor and is eaten fresh. Mashed, strained and mixed into milk, the pulp makes a superb tropical drink. Sugar Apple may be grown from seed or may be grafted onto Custard Apple or Pond Apple rootstock. It is grown extensively in India, where it has been introduced. It withstands drought better than most other fruit trees.

POND APPLE
Annona glabra

NATIVE: South Florida and Caribbean.
FAMILY: Annonaceae.
ZONES: S

Small, fast-growing evergreen tree native to American tropics and south Florida, growing up to 40 feet in height. Leaves are bright green, oval-shaped, 4–6 inches long. Flowers are creamy-white or greenish-white with red centers, about an inch wide. They are followed in late summer by smooth, yellow-skinned fruits, 2–4 inches long, with large brown, bean-like seeds imbedded in yellowish-white pulp. Although edible, the pulp is dry and has an unappetizing flavor similar to that of wild mangoes. A swamp-lover, Pond Apple is found in low areas. Large stands once stood south of Lake Okeechobee. It is sometimes called Custard Apple, though that term more often refers to *A. reticulata* (above). FLORIDA HABITAT: Hardwood swamp forests and cypress swamp forests.

SOURSOP

Annona muricata

NATIVE: Central America.
FAMILY: Annonaceae.

ZONES: S

Also called Guanabana. This small tropical tree seldom grows over 20 feet in height. It has a slender trunk and scraggly branches. Leathery, deep green leaves are 3–4 inches long and exude a pungent odor when crushed. Round, fleshy, white flowers with 3 sepals and 6 petals are borne on short stems. The oddly misshapen fruit is 8–10 inches long and 5 inches wide with green skin. It is covered by soft, fleshy spines and often grows directly on the trunk of the tree. In the delicious, cottony-white pulp are embedded shiny black, bean-shaped seeds. Soursop prefers acid, sandy soil and requires supplemental irrigation during dry periods. It can survive short periods of cold weather without serious harm.

LOQUAT

Eriobotrya japonica

EXOTIC: China, Japan.
FAMILY: Rosaceae.

ZONES: N, C, S

Growing to about 20 feet in height, this small evergreen tree is popular and easily grown throughout the state. Nurseries sell many different cultivars, which may be labeled "Japanese Plum". Leaves are 4–8 inches long, dark green above, tan and downy underneath. Its small, white, sweet-scented flowers, borne in fall or winter, may justify its use as an ornamental, but additionally, the fruits that follow are considered a delicacy. The 2- inch long, plum-like, yellowish-orange fruit may be eaten raw or made into pies or preserves. The Loquat thrives in almost any soil, is drought tolerant and fairly salt tolerant. It probably needs the least attention of any tree grown in Florida for fruit.

PAPAYA

Carica papaya

EXOTIC: Mexico.
FAMILY: Caricaceae.

ZONES: S

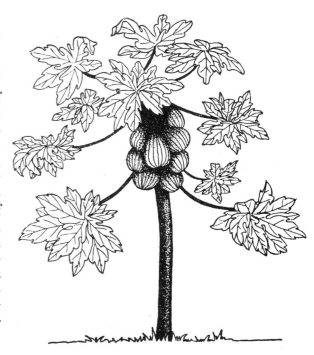

Though not a tree, this 15- to 18-foot tall annual is one of south Florida's most common backyard tropical fruits. Its huge, lobed leaves (1½–2 feet wide) grow at right angles to the trunk. They are dark green above, lighter green below. Fragrant male and female flowers are borne year-round on separate plants. Small yellowish-white male flowers grow in clusters on long, drooping stems; inch-wide female flowers, waxy white with yellow centers, appear at each leaf axil. Pollination is by sphinx moths. Ripe fruits weigh from one to several pounds. Fruit is sweet and aromatic, and contains many round, slippery seeds. Papayas contain papain, a milky substance used commercially to make meat tenderizer. If it escapes frost, a plant may persist for several years, but its fruit will usually be of poor quality. Strictly an oasis plant, Papaya has little tolerance for drought, nor for salt air.

EDIBLE FIG
Ficus carica

EXOTIC: Asia.
FAMILY: Moraceae.
ZONES: N, C, S

Figs are grown commercially in California and states bordering the Gulf of Mexico, but not in Florida. In Florida, fig trees rarely exceed 20 feet. Unlike the leaves of most trees in the *Ficus* genus, the leaves are shaped like the palm of the hand. They are dull green above with whitish-green, downy undersides. Minute, unisexual flowers are borne inside pear-shaped receptacles growing close to the branches. After flowers are pollinated this receptacle develops into a 2- to 3-inch long, sweet-flavored fruit. Fig trees will make a dense growth in good, well-drained soil, but tend to become scraggly in dry, sandy locations. Propagation is from cuttings, with trees bearing the first year. They are often grown in pots as well. Brown Turkey, Brunswick, Magnolia and Celeste are varieties most often grown in Florida.

CARAMBOLA
Averrhoa carambola

EXOTIC: Malaysia.
FAMILY: Oxalidaceae.
ZONES: S

Since the unusual fruit of this tree began appearing in markets, more people are including it in their landscapes. Rarely more than 30 feet tall and evergreen, its compound leaves are made up of 5–11 paper-thin, light green leaflets which fold up at night. Small, pink, 5-petalled, fragrant flowers are produced in spring and summer with the yellow-orange, waxy fruit ripening summer through winter. Fruit is about 4 inches long and egg-shaped overall, with 5 or 6 longitudinal ridges which form a characteristic star shape when the fruit is cross-sectioned. Fruits may grow at the ends of twigs, or sometimes are attached directly to the trunk of the tree. Several cultivars are available to Florida growers in our frost free and salt free areas. Established trees may require some irrigation during extended periods of drought. Carambola is propagated by seeds, air layering or grafting.

JABOTICABA
Myrciaria cauliflora

EXOTIC: Brazil.
FAMILY: Myrtaceae.
ZONES: S

Rather slow growing, this 10- to 15-foot tree does not bear for several years, but once it begins to produce it blooms and offers delicious fruit, often in great quantities, almost year round. The time from flower to fruit is only a month. Small wine-colored fruits, shiny and grape-like, grow singly or in twos or threes, either directly on the trunk or on twigs. Thick, tough skin covers the juicy white pulp, which tastes rather like grapes. Fruit is eaten fresh or made into jelly or wine. Jaboticaba is evergreen and withstands temperatures below freezing for short periods. Grafted plants from nurseries and the use of adequate water and fertilizer make for maximum harvest.

LYCHEE
Litchi chinensis

Exotic: Asia.
Family: Sapindaceae.
Zones: S

The Lychee has been cultivated in Asia for at least 2000 years, in Florida for a few decades. It thrives on humidity but does not tolerate prolonged cold. Lychee grows as far north along the Gulf Coast as St. Petersburg. Often called "Lychee-Nut," that term properly refers to the dried fruit. Under optimal conditions, these trees are long-lived; many have lived to be hundreds of years old. A handsome 25-foot tall tree, with glossy, dark green leaves hanging pendulum fashion, it would be worth its space as a shade tree even if it did not bear fruit. Small greenish-white flowers grow in clusters 6–8 inches long, with iridescent red fruit ripening in June. Oval-shaped fruits an inch in diameter grow in grape-like clusters. Their pulp, creamy-white, juicy and pleasant tasting, is contained in a shell that is rough, brittle and thin. Propagation is by seed, air layering or grafting; the hard, round, tan seeds are pea-sized. A number of varieties are available from nurseries.

LONGAN
Euphoria longana

Exotic: India.
Family: Sapindaceae.
Zones: S

As a beautiful, 30-foot tall evergreen, the Longan is often grown as a shade tree. It is closely related to the Lychee and is similar in appearance. The 3- to 6-inch leaves are glossy green, but new flushes of growth may be varicolored. Inconspicuous white flowers are borne in spring, in clusters 5–7 inches long. The Longan's pleasantly tart fruit is pebbled, brown-skinned with white flesh, and ripens in late summer or fall. It may be eaten fresh, dried or preserved. Although the Longan is said to be hardier than the Lychee, both trees are definitely tropical and can withstand only short periods of freezing. Both can be propagated by seeds, but grafting is desirable for best fruit. The Longan is not salt tolerant, but is fairly drought tolerant.

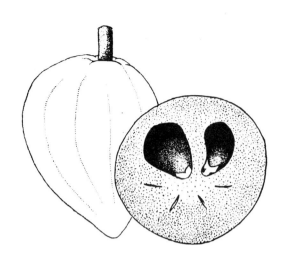

EGGFRUIT — *Pouteria campechiana*

EXOTIC: Mexico and Central America.
FAMILY: Sapotaceae.   ZONES: S

Also called Canistel. The musky-flavored fruit of this small tree is relished by many people, but others find it disagreeably sweet. The Eggfruit tree rapidly reaches about 25 feet in height and has a spreading growth habit. Its brittle wood is subject to wind damage if not kept pruned. Leathery, bright green leaves are oblong with pointed tips. Incon-spicuous white flowers are followed by 3- to 4-inch long, yellowish-orange, round to egg-shaped fruits, each tipped with a sharp beak. The fruit's paper-thin outer skin encloses mealy pulp the color and consistency of a hard-boiled egg yolk. Each fruit contains one or more brown seeds. Eggfruit may be eaten raw, or made into custard or sherbet.

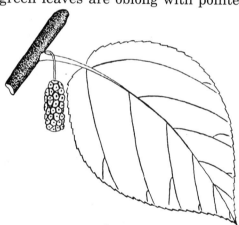

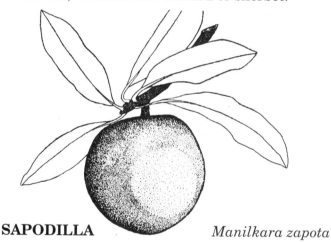

RED MULBERRY — *Morus rubra*

NATIVE: Eastern and Central United States.
FAMILY: Moraceae.   ZONES: N, C, S

This fast-growing deciduous tree grows to 60 feet in height. Its wide, rounded crown tops a thick, sturdy trunk with grayish-brown bark. Leaves are variable in form, occasionally lobed but usually heart-shaped; they are 3–7 inches long, dark green above, yellowish-green beneath. Tiny, inconspicuous male and female flowers are borne in separate catkins on the same tree. Edible fruit, 1½ inches long, is bright red, becoming purplish-black when fully ripe. It has a pleasant, subacid flavor. This long-lived tree requires full sun, is easily propagated from cuttings, and is a wonderful bird attractor. FLORIDA HABITAT: Hydric hammocks, upland mesic hardwood forests, pineland forests.

SAPODILLA — *Manilkara zapota*

EXOTIC: Mexico and Central America.
FAMILY: Sapotaceae.   ZONES: S

This large, handsome, evergreen tree reaches 50 feet in height, with a rounded crown of dense foliage. Leaves are stiff, leathery, dark glossy green, 2–5 inches long, and grow in clusters at the end of short branches. Small, creamy-white flowers are followed by brownish, round fruits, 2–4 inches in diameter, with thin, scurfy skin and yellowish-brown, transparent pulp that is spicy-sweet when ripe. Fruit is best when eaten raw. Sapodilla is very susceptible to cold injury, but in extreme south Florida it is popular as a shade tree and produces fruits irregularly throughout the year. A white latex, chicle, is obtained from the tree and its green fruit; it is used in the manufacture of chewing gum.

AMERICAN PERSIMMON *Diospyros virginiana*

NATIVE: Eastern United States.
FAMILY: Ebenaceae.   ZONES: N, C, S

This deciduous, hardwood American tree is widely distributed throughout the Eastern United States. It grows wild in many places, but is also cultivated for its fruit. Forty feet tall, it has spreading branches and a short, stocky trunk a foot or more in diameter. Thick brown bark is usually covered with scaly oblong patches separated by deep crevices. Dark green leaves, polished and leathery, have pale undersides and may be up to 6 inches long. Dried, they can be used to make tea. Small, bell-shaped, white or greenish-yellow flowers are borne in the axils of leaves in spring. Separate trees produce male and female blossoms; cross-pollination is required for fruit. Smooth-skinned fruit is yellow and plum-like; it ripens in late summer or early fall. Extremely astringent when green, when fully mature it becomes yellowish-orange, sweet and pulpy, with 3–5 flat brown seeds embedded in its flesh. American Permission can be propagated by seed or by transplanting the small suckers that emerge from the base of the trunk. To maintain a tree-like form, these suckers should be removed periodically. Several species of Asian persimmons are cultivated here for their fruit (one is *D. kaki*), which is much larger than that of the American species.

TAMARIND   *Tamarindus indica*

EXOTIC: India.
FAMILY: Leguminosae.   ZONES: S

Introduced into Florida nearly 250 years ago, this evergreen tree is cultivated throughout the tropical world. It grows to a height of 45 feet or more, with an enormous, dense crown. Feathery, 6-inch long leaves have 12 or more pairs of inch-long, light green, oval leaflets; these close at night. Yellowish-white flowers are touched with red and are borne in clusters. Each has 3 large and 2 small petals. Fruit is a bean-like pod that contains seeds surrounded by an acid pulp with a sweet-tart flavor. This pulp, used for preserves and also in Worcestershire sauce, is very high in vitamin B and calcium. Tamarind thrives only in frost-free south Florida, where it is planted for its fruit and as an ornamental. Its strong wood makes it extremely resistant to wind; it is very drought tolerant and tolerates some salt. It can be propagated by seed.

SATIN LEAF
Chrysophyllum oliviforme

NATIVE: Everglades and Florida Keys.
FAMILY: Sapotaceae.   ZONES: S

The common and scientific names of this medium-sized tree comes from its leaves, which are shiny green above, copper-colored and velvety below. When blown by the breeze, both colors are evident. Satin Leaf may grow as tall as 35 feet; its reddish-brown trunk has fissured bark. Leaves are 2–4 inches long, oval in shape with pointed tips. Insignificant, greenish- or yellowish-white flowers have 5 petals and appear in fall. Deep purple, 3/4-inch long fruit has a single seed; slightly sweet and juicy, it may be used to make jelly. It resembles an olive in appearance, which accounts for the species name. Satin Leaf is a slow-growing tree that requires little water or fertilizer and tolerates some salt. However, it is not particularly cold hardy and is best cultivated in south Florida or in coastal areas free from frost. It may be propagated by seed. FLORIDA HABITAT: Maritime forests and rockland hammocks of south Florida.

BANANA
Musa spp.

EXOTIC: Southeast Asia.
FAMILY: Musaceae.   ZONES: S

Although some may reach 30 feet in height, Banana plants are not trees, but herbaceous perennials. A number of varieties can be grown in south Florida, some of these cultivated for their bright flowers, others for their delicious fruit. *Musa acuminata,* its cultivars, or hybrids are most often grown for fruit. All bananas need a warm climate, moist, well-drained soil and adequate fertilizer rich in potassium. Given these things, they are easy to grow and reward the grower with great bunches of sweet fruit. The small Cavendish or Lady Finger bananas are sweeter than the larger ones sold in supermarkets throughout the country; those imported varieties are favored commercially for their transportability and slow ripening qualities rather than their palatability. The Plantain is a banana hybrid with firmer, less-sweet flesh and is usually eaten cooked. Banana species grown for their flowers include *M. ornata* (lavender), *M. velutina* (pink), and *M. coccinea* (red). *M. zebrina* has red flowers also, as well as edible fruit and attractive foliage; it is a blue-green color above, red below. Banana stalks die soon after fruiting, but each dying stalk is usually replaced by several new suckers.

Bibliography

Association of Florida Native Nurseries, Inc. *Xeric Landscaping with Florida Native Plants*, Hollywood, FL: Betrock Information Systems, Inc., 1991.

Broschat, Timothy K., and Alan W. Meerow. *Betrock's Reference Guide to Florida Landscape Plants*. Hollywood, FL: Betrock Information Systems, Inc., 1991.

Carr, Archie. *The Everglades, The American Wilderness* (series). Alexandria, VA: Time-Life Books, 1973.

Cerulean, Susan, Celeste Botha and Donna Legare. *Planting a Refuge for Wildlife: How to create a backyard habitat for Florida's birds and beasts*. Tallahassee: Florida Game and Freshwater Fish Commission, 1987.

Huegel, Craig. *Butterfly Gardening with Florida's Native Plants*. Orlando: Florida Native Plant Society, 1991.

Long, Robert W., and Olga Lakela, *A Flora of Tropical Florida*. Coral Gables: University of Miami Press, 1971.

Menninger, Edwin A. *Flowering Trees of the World*. New York: Hearthside Press, 1962.

Myers, Ronald L., and John J. Ewel, ed. *Ecosystems of Florida*, Orlando: University of Central Florida Press, 1990.

Nelson, Gil. *The Trees of Florida: A Reference and Field Guide*. Sarasota, FL: Pineapple Press, 1994.

Popenoe, Wilson. *Manual of Tropical and Subtropical Fruits*. New York: Hafner Press, 1948.

Schuetz, Maxine. *Flowering Trees for Central and South Florida Gardens*. St. Petersburg, FL: Great Outdoors Publishing Co., 1990.

Scurlock, J. Paul. *Native Trees and Shrubs of the Florida Keys*. Bethel Park, PA: Laurel Press, 1987.

Stresau, Frederic B. *Florida, My Eden*. Port Salerno, FL: Florida Classics Library, 1986.

Sturrock, David. *Fruits for Southern Florida*, Stuart, FL: Southeastern Printing Co., 1959.

Watkins, John V., and Thomas J. Sheehan. *Florida Landscape Plants*, Revised Edition. Gainesville: University Presses of Florida, 1975.

Zucker, Isabel. *Flowering Shrubs and Small Trees*. New York: Grove Weidenfeld, 1990.

Botanical Gardens in Florida

Arboretum at UCF
University of Central Florida
Orlando, FL 32816

Bok Tower Gardens
1151 Tower Boulevard
Lake Wales, FL 33853

Butterfly World
3600 West Sample Road
Coconut Creek, FL 33073

Cypress Gardens
2641 South Lake Summit Drive
Winter Haven, FL 33884

Eureka Springs Botanical Garden
6400 Eureka Springs Road
Tampa, FL 33620

Fairchild Tropical Garden
10901 Old Cutler Road
Miami, FL 33158-4233

Flamingo Gardens
3750 Flamingo Road
Fort Lauderdale, FL 33330

Gizella Kopsick Palm Arboretum
North Shore Drive
St. Petersburg, FL

Kanapaha Botanical Gardens
4625 SW 63rd Boulevard
Gainesville, FL 32608

Leu Botanical Gardens
1730 North Forest Avenue
Orlando, FL 32803

Maclay State Gardens
3540 Thomasville Road
Tallahassee, FL 32308

Marie Selby Botanical Gardens
811 South Palm Avenue
Sarasota, FL 34236

Morikami Museum, Gardens & Park
400 Morikami Road
Delray Beach, FL 33446

Mount's Botanical Garden
531 North Military Trail
West Palm Beach, FL 33415

Parrot Jungle
11000 SW 57th Avenue
Miami, FL 33156

Ravine State Gardens
1500 Twigg Street
Palatka, FL 32178

Redlands Fruit & Spice Park
24801 SW 187th Avenue
Homestead, FL 33030

Sarasota Jungle Gardens
3701 Bayshore Road
Sarasota, FL 34234

Sugar Mill Gardens
Herbert Street
Port Orange, FL

Thomas Edison Home
2350 McGregor Boulevard
Fort Myers, FL 33901

USF Botanical Garden
University of South Florida
4202 Fowler Avenue
Tampa, FL 33606

Vizcaya Museum and Gardens
3251 S Miami Avenue
Miami, FL 33129

Washington Oaks State Gardens
6400 Oceanshore Boulevard
Palm Coast, FL 32137

Index